Life-Situation Preaching for African-Americans

Life-Situation Preaching for African-Americans

Willie J. Newton Jr.

Foreword by Frank A. Thomas

◆PICKWICK *Publications* • Eugene, Oregon

LIFE-SITUATION PREACHING FOR AFRICAN-AMERICANS

Copyright © 2019 Willie J. Newton Jr. All rights reserved. Except for brief quotations in critical publications or reviews, no part of this book may be reproduced in any manner without prior written permission from the publisher. Write: Permissions, Wipf and Stock Publishers, 199 W. 8th Ave., Suite 3, Eugene, OR 97401.

Pickwick Publications
An Imprint of Wipf and Stock Publishers
199 W. 8th Ave., Suite 3
Eugene, OR 97401

www.wipfandstock.com

PAPERBACK ISBN: 978-1-5326-5497-8
HARDCOVER ISBN: 978-1-5326-5498-5
EBOOK ISBN: 978-1-5326-5499-2

Cataloguing-in-Publication data:

Names: Newton, Willie J., Jr., author.

Title: Life-situation preaching for African-Americans / Willie J. Newton Jr.

Description: Eugene, OR: Pickwick Publications, 2019 | Includes bibliographical references and index.

Identifiers: ISBN 978-1-5326-5497-8 (paperback). | ISBN 978-1-5326-5498-5 (hardcover). | ISBN 978-1-5326-5499-2 (ebook).

Subjects: LCSH: African-American preaching. | Preaching—United States. | Fosdick, Harry Emerson, 1878–1969.

Classification: BV4221 N 2019 (paperback). | BV4221 (ebook).

Manufactured in the U.S.A.   12/10/19

Unless otherwise noted, Scripture quotations are from the New Revised Standard Version Bible, copyright © 1989 National Council of the Churches of Christ in the United States of America. Used by permission. All rights reserved worldwide.

Contents

Foreword by Frank A. Thomas | vii
Preface | xi
Acknowledgments | xiii
Introduction | xv

1 Fosdick's Life and Early Ministry | 1

2 The Nature of Life-Situation Preaching | 21

3 Fosdick's Preaching Ministry | 62

4 Strengths and Weaknesses of Fosdick's Life-Situation Preaching | 77

5 The Christian Vocation and Life-Situation Preaching | 100

6 Preaching to African-Americans' Life Situations | 112

Bibliography | 131

Foreword

I am excited that in the second decade of the twenty-first century we have entered a golden age of the study and publication of works on and about the study and concerns of African-American preaching. Initially, beginning with Henry H. Mitchell's *Black Preaching* in 1970, African-American preachers began speaking to the theological academic world to take seriously the art, genius, power, history, imagination, and depth of black preaching. From the roots of Mitchell's seminal work, the tree of African-American preaching has grown to have full and rich branches. *Life-Situation Preaching for African-Americans* by Willie J. Newton Jr. is an excellent example of the level of rich and diverse branches of the study of African-American preaching. As Newton notes, the study of African-American preaching has moved well beyond contrasting African-American preaching and Euro-American preaching to texts that study many and varied interesting aspects of preaching in general, and black preaching in particular. Newton chooses an intersectional topic: the twentieth-century life-situation preaching of Harry Emerson Fosdick that can help enhance the life-situation preaching of African-Americans in the twenty-first century.

Newton does several things that are critically important in this book. First, he does a thorough analysis of the preaching of Harry Emerson Fosdick. Fosdick was one of the most iconic and prolific preachers of the twentieth century and the pastor of the Riverside Church of New York City for forty years. Newton confirmed Fosdick's stature among African-American preachers by suggesting his influence on three giants of the African-American pulpit: Martin Luther King Jr, Benjamin Elijah Mays, and Samuel DeWitt Proctor. Newton rightly suggests: "If men of such distinction and high caliber consulted Fosdick's printed materials for sermonic ideas, then there must be something of immeasurable worth in Fosdick's life-situation preaching

Foreword

and Christian ministry." It is always beneficial to have a serious study of the preaching method of any great preacher of any age, race, ethnicity, or gender. To have the method, process, strengths and weaknesses of such a prodigious preacher as Harry Emerson Fosdick is a goldmine for preachers who want to improve their craft. We are deeply indebted to Newton for this impartial foray into such a great preacher that we all might preach better.

Second, in order to dialogue between Fosdick and African-American preaching, there must be a thorough analysis of African-American preaching. Newton defines and characterizes African-American preaching and presents a summary of African-American preaching. It is hard to find a concise summary of Henry H. Mitchell, James Earl Massey, Gardner C. Taylor, Frank A. Thomas, Cleophus J. LaRue, Teresa Fry Brown, and Lisa L. Thompson in one place. This alone is worth the price of the book. The summary analysis of black preaching is worth the purchase price of the book alone. Newton helps those of us who teach and preach African-American preaching and those who desire to learn of it to better understand our tradition.

Thirdly, Newton is on to something important in his understanding of life-situation preaching. I direct the world's first and only PhD Program in African-American Preaching and Sacred Rhetoric. We have ten students working profusely to complete the program and write and teach and add their contribution to the field of preaching and African-American preaching. In our classes, we study the theology and methods of African-American preaching and otherwise. After we studied the field, then I asked them about their theology and method of African-American preaching. One of the exercises that I took them through was the Wesleyan Quadrilateral and its four component parts of Scripture, Tradition, Reason, and Experience. I asked them in their method of sermon preparation which comes first. Does Scripture, Tradition, Reason, or Experience come first? At first, their response was the politically correct response that Scripture comes first. But then as we discussed it in greater detail, two of them said, "Experience and the life situation of the hearers comes first, and then Scriptures." Initially, I was hesitant because I was trained to believe that Scripture and exegesis to ascertain as close as we can the original meaning of the text is the beginning point for preaching. Despite my protestation, they firmly and honestly claimed the life situation of the hearers as the starting point. Not all of them said this, but several did. Their comments forced me to go home and reexamine my assumption that I utilized Scripture and exegesis first, and I discovered, more than I had paid attention to, that several of my

Foreword

sermons start with the life situations of the audience. I believe that Newton has addressed a contemporary phenomenon in preaching that we will be hearing more and more about. Of course, there are critics and traditionalists, including me, who believe the sermon starts with and is organized by the biblical text. But I am open to the discussion because at least a few of my sermons start with the life situation of the hearer. Some would even argue that we bring our life situation to the biblical text and exegesis. But that is more discussion for another time.

Finally, I would offer one other key point that I would not like the reader to miss that Newton offers in discussing the strong connection between African-American preaching and the life-situation preaching of Fosdick. Newton recounts that Fosdick believed that preaching and pastoral counseling were not two distinct functions, but "indispensable offices of one vocational task; inseparably conjoined in one office." It has been long discussed among preachers that Fosdick approached the pulpit as though he was beginning a personal counseling session. Fosdick believed that pastoral counseling and preaching were vital one to another. Counseling hours provided deep insights into human nature that translates into relevant content for preaching. Newton recounts Fosdick: "the right kind of preacher is coerced to become a personal counselor, and the right kind of personal counselor gains some of the most necessary ingredients of preaching." Newton confirms, establishes, and extrapolates on this as fact to the immense help of many pastors who encounter the life situations of their congregations every day in their offices. In my experience as an African-American preacher and pastor, my preaching was deeply influenced by what I heard in the pastoral sessions with congregants.

Without a doubt, I recommend this book to African-American and non-African-American preacher alike. I have highlighted some of the lessons to be gained, and in reading it you will discover even more. I am grateful for this branch that integrates the African-American preaching tradition with the work of Harry Emerson Fosdick. It will help all of us become better preachers.

Frank A. Thomas
Director PhD Program African-American Preaching and Sacred Rhetoric
Christian Theological Seminary
Indianapolis, Indiana

Preface

This analysis of the benefits of Harry Emerson Fosdick's (1878–1969) life-situation preaching for African-Americans is an eye-opening exploration into the preaching excellence of a once-iconic American preacher. Given Fosdick's successful preaching ministry and his effective approach to preaching, his advice to young preachers and novice preachers is worth revisiting. Every Sunday such preachers stand before an awaiting congregation to preach the Gospel and more than one of these preachers feel disenchanted with the chosen approach to preaching and its lack of response from the listeners. Consequently, the preacher is disenchanted, and the congregation is disengaged.

One of the problems is that the preacher's approach to preaching is ill-suited for the congregational context, especially as it relates to African-American contexts. Unless one attends a historically African-American theological institution such as Howard University School of Divinity (Washington, DC), the Samuel Dewitt Proctor School of Theology of Virginia University (Richmond, VA), or Shaw University Divinity School (Raleigh, NC), to note a few examples, the preacher is not likely to encounter approaches to preaching that are effective for and consistent with African-American worship contexts. Such efforts as those of the Christian Theological Seminary (Indianapolis, IN) to develop scholar-practitioners of preaching through its PhD in African-American Preaching and Sacred Rhetoric are to be highly appreciated and commended. This program is the first of its kind in the world. Frank A. Thomas, an authority on African-American preaching, professor of homiletics, and author of several books on preaching, is the director of the program.

The title *Life-Situation Preaching for African-Americans* is somewhat misleading in that much of so-called African-American preaching is life-situation preaching. While I am not a homiletician, I have been practicing

Preface

the art of preaching for twenty years. I understand the frustration of not being able to connect with listeners because of intransigent fidelity to an approach, which precludes one from touching on issues of vital concern to listeners. This book recognizes the need for young preachers and novice preachers within the African-American preaching context to practice an approach to preaching that is true to their personality and pastoral identity. There is no universal or uniform approach to preaching; approaches are as multifaceted as the women and men who use them. Generally speaking, the discipline of homiletics is a Euro-American dominated enterprise that is taught from Euro-centric perspectives, with few notable exceptions. The homiletics courses taught in Euro-American seminaries and divinity schools assign African-American authors and homileticians as supplemental readings to increase situational awareness, not to provide alternative approaches to preaching.

The urgent need of the church today is well-trained, well-disciplined preachers who take seriously the Great Commission found in the Gospel of Matthew 28:19–20: "Go therefore and make disciples of all nations, baptizing them in the name of the Father and of the Son and of the Holy Spirit, and teaching them to obey everything that I have commanded you. And remember, I am with you always, to the end of the age. To meet the demands of such a commission calls for staying power and preaching power. The former is the power to stick with it during difficult times, while the latter is the ability to preach, accompanied by the aid of the Holy Spirit, with extraordinary force. The approach to preaching espoused in this book is for the preacher who wants to meet the personal and social needs of those to whom she preaches. Having insight into the personal and social dynamics of people's lives translates into data for life-situation preaching. A listener of a sermon need not subsequently forage for spiritual food if the preacher is sufficiently nourishing the listener with the life-giving, life-sustaining spiritual and intellectual substance of the word of God. The preacher must be able to address the challenges and struggles that ordinary people face daily. This is especially true in relation to the unique experiences of African-Americans. Life-situation preaching helps with this undertaking.

Acknowledgments

This book would not have materialized without the steady support and encouragement of many people who have contributed directly or indirectly its composition. The names are too numerous to recount here. I would be unforgivably remiss, though, if I did not mention a few.

I thank my Yale Divinity School teacher, Clifton Granby, for challenging me to think more deeply about the particularities of African-Americans' life situations. The quintessential mentor and friend, he devoted charitable time to critical dialogue regarding the historical significance and implications of African-American religious and political thought for our modern times.

I am grateful to Frank A. Thomas for reading early versions of the manuscripts and for writing the foreword. Thomas, a consummate practitioner-scholar, is in the business of developing and mentoring practitioners and scholars who not only preach skillfully, but also are capable of graduate-level research and rigorous analysis.

I thank William H. Willimon, former Dean of Duke Chapel and Professor of the Practice of Christian Ministry at Duke Divinity School, for his helpful criticisms of early drafts. A prolific writer and gifted preacher, he made this book much better than it would have been otherwise.

I owe a considerable debt of gratitude to Rufus Burrow Jr., Distinguished Visiting Professor of Theological Social Ethics and Black Church Leadership at United Theological Seminary of the Twin Cities, a fine gentleman and scholar in his own right, who painstakingly and patiently edited multiple drafts of this book, making it a worthwhile undertaking for the author and, I hope, the reader.

Although these esteemed gentlemen have assisted in making this book worthy of publication and, most importantly, worthy of readership, I take full responsibility for the views and errors herein.

Acknowledgments

I extend my heartfelt thanks to family and friends who have supported and encouraged me along the way, while tolerating my absence from important life events.

Introduction

There is an urgent need for such a book. One need only to visit a local church on any given Sunday to determine its urgency. It is too often the case that contemporary preaching does not get at the personal and social problems that people face. Ineffective and irrelevant preaching has plagued much of today's preaching enterprise. Preaching matters! What is said or left unsaid in the pulpit matters. I am convinced that the epidemic of empty church pews originated with empty content in the pulpit. Preachers should be concerned. The church community should be worried. But we need not be without hope. There is hope and help for the preacher desiring an approach to preaching that brings the preacher close to the vital issues that affect listeners of sermons. Life-situation preaching is such an approach. This approach provides the preacher with an approach that starts with listeners' vital practical needs and offers a practical solution.

In this book I discuss some of the strengths, weaknesses, and implications of Harry Emerson Fosdick's *life-situation preaching* for young preachers and novice preachers in so-called mainline churches in general and African-American ones in particular.[1] Fosdick, like most people of his era,

---

1. I contend that all preaching that speaks to life situations can fall under the umbrella of life-situation preaching. African-American preaching is not an exception to the rule. In fact, African-American preaching is life-situation preaching, and life-situation preaching is African-American preaching. However, life-situation preaching in this book extends beyond Fosdick's life-situation preaching. That is to say, life-situation preaching as it is understood herein consists of the best practices of the Euro-American and African-American preaching traditions. The benefit of this approach is that it recognizes and overcomes the limitations inherent in each tradition to forge a more excellent homiletic. As regards mainline churches, in *The Black Church in the African-American Experience*, C. Eric Lincoln's and Lawrence H. Mamiya's operational definition of "the black church" is limited to seven independent, historic denominations or mainline churches: three Methodists, three Baptists, and the Churches of God in Christ (COGIC). I use the words "black" and "African-American" interchangeably throughout this book. The major factor

Introduction

used the term "mainline" in reference to white mainline churches, such as Disciples, Presbyterians, United Methodists, Episcopalians, and Baptists. While the focus of this book is on mainline churches, most, if not all, of these problems adversely affect non-mainline churches as well.

Fosdick was an iconic figure in American religious and cultural life. Arguably, he was the most eminent and controversial preacher of his day, particularly in white church circles. A liberal Christian pastor, famed radio personality, prolific author and respected professor, Fosdick's preaching attracted large crowds. He founded the Riverside Church in New York City, a nondenominational, nonsectarian church, where he remained for forty years, preaching every Sunday to three thousand listeners. People were spellbound by his oratorical prowess, puzzled by his unorthodox theology, and fascinated by his vast literary interests. Martin Luther King Jr. had tremendous respect and admiration for Fosdick. Appreciatively, King sent Fosdick a personally inscribed copy of his political autobiography *Stride Toward Freedom*, with more than modest comment: "If I were called upon to select the greatest preacher of this century, I would choose your name. If I were called upon to select the foremost prophets of our generation, I would choose you to head the list. If I were called upon to select the Christian saints of our day, again I would have to place you on the list. Because of all these things and the inspiration that youve [sic] been to me, I present you with this book."[2] King was most appreciative of Fosdick's preaching ministry, both orally and literarily. This inscription provides one with a sense of King's high admiration and appreciation for Fosdick's preaching ministry.

At the heart of Fosdick's successful ministry was his practical approach to preaching, which was the result of various intersecting characteristics of his life. His personal and religious experiences, his endless quest for knowledge, and his personal consultation practices, all contributed immeasurably to his theory of preaching and his pastoral identity. It was, however, his discontentment and frustration with the then-current approaches to preaching that prompted his experimentation with life-situation preaching. He called his approach "project preaching" or the "project method." Contemporary preachers refer to Fosdick's approach as "life-situation"

---

that indicates which is preferred is the way in which the words are used and referenced by the authors quoted or referenced in this book. The same is true for the words "white," "European American," or "of European descent," etc.

2. Carson et al., eds., *Papers*, 4:536. King's inscription to Fosdick, November 17, 1958.

Introduction

preaching, although he himself never used this language. Herein I use this term to describe and analyze his preaching.

Fosdick's departure from the aforementioned approaches to preaching resulted in a radically different approach that placed people's life situations as the starting point of the sermon. Such is the point of departure for a Fosdick sermon. He structured his sermons according to the problem-solution format, wherein he stated a problem or need, advocated a solution, and aimed at actuation. It should be noted that he truly desired to help people, and this is precisely why he started his sermons with the lived experiences of everyday people, attempting to better understand, interpret, and preach to their life situations. Exploring all available resources, especially the Bible, Fosdick directed his preaching toward people's personal and social problems.

A salient theme in Fosdick's published works was his message to young preachers in mainline churches, urging them to address the needs of their people. Many contemporary readers know little about Fosdick's life, the factors that guided him to Christian ministry, and the factors that led him to life-situation preaching. Although Fosdick's life-situation approach to preaching is unfamiliar to many contemporary preachers, I believe that his approach has merits that are well worth revisiting, especially from the perspective outlined in this book. As implied before, my aim is to bring Fosdick's thought into dialogue with contemporary preaching and present-day African-American issues. No historical or contemporary work has attempted to do this. My intention here is to help fill this void.

My concern is twofold. I am concerned with the advantages and benefits of life-situation preaching for young African-American preachers, pastors, and seminarians, and I am concerned with the preacher of any ethnicity who is accountable to African-American listeners. I do not assume that only African-American preachers preach to African-American listeners. It is true that some predominantly African-American churches have a non-African-American preacher, and it is also true that some predominately white churches have an African-American preacher. Examples abound. It is worth noting that I am not concerned with various forms or theories of African-American preaching as compared with Eurocentric preaching. This is not a technical manual on the theory, history, principles, and techniques of African-American preaching. Many distinguished African-American homileticians (Henry H. Mitchel, James Earl Massey, Katie

Introduction

Geneva Cannon, Frank A. Thomas, Cleophus J. LaRue) have authored phenomenal books on the subject.

The argument of this book is based on a consideration of Fosdick's major works and that of select life-situation proponents. Fosdick's writings on sermon composition and delivery are indispensable to what follows. Although different perspectives are considered, the primary focus is on Fosdick's thinking regarding life-situation preaching as a means to address the issues that are disrupting lives, troubling minds, and burdening consciences. While it is true that life-situation preaching has some weaknesses, most notably its starting point of the listeners' problems as opposed to starting with the Bible, it is also true that it provides an effective approach to preaching for young and novice preachers of African-American listeners when used intelligently and creatively.

To gain a proper appreciation for Fosdick, the reader must understand that Fosdick was a man of ideas who believed in the infinite power of an *idea*. Ideas, he reasoned, are potent instruments of familial, societal, and communal transformation. The right idea at the right time can save lives, transform lives, prevent crises, and improve the quality of everyday life. He once sermonized that people come and go but ideas abide.[3] An idea outlasts its originator. The spirit of an idea moves from one person to another, from one generation to another. Restless spirit, an idea uses an individual for a while, even a lifetime, and then it moves on to another host.

Richard Lischer has documented unattributed uses of Fosdick's ideas and printed materials. Fosdick's sermonic content featured prominently in the public discourses of Benjamin E. Mays, Samuel Proctor, and Martin Luther King Jr, for example. These preachers were some of the best that the African-American pulpit had to offer. If men of such distinction and high caliber consulted Fosdick's printed materials for sermonic ideas, then there must be something of immeasurable worth in Fosdick's life-situation preaching and Christian ministry.

Chapter 1, "Fosdick's Life and Early Ministry," provides an overview of the significant personal and religious experiences that shaped Fosdick's life and ministry. Chapter 2, "The Nature of Life-Situation Preaching," examines the nature of life-situation preaching and its relationship with pastoral counseling. It also explores similarities between African-American preaching and life-situation preaching. Chapters 3, "Fosdick's Preaching Ministry," and 4, "Strengths and Weaknesses of Fosdick's Life-Situation

---

3. See Fosdick, "The Ideas That Use Us," 171–179.

Introduction

Preaching," give attention to Fosdick's theory and practice of preaching and its strengths and weaknesses. Chapter 5, "The Christian Vocation and Life-Situation Preaching," discusses Fosdick's advice to young Christian ministers and the implications of life-situation preaching for contemporary practitioners. In Chapter 6, "Preaching to African-Americans' Life Situations," the final chapter of this book, I discuss some of the benefits of life-situation preaching for African-American listeners. It is the author's hope that the ideas presented in this book will seize you fiercely and set you ablaze with renewed energy and enthusiasm for preaching.

1

Fosdick's Life and Early Ministry

Fosdick's Organic Ingredients

Every preacher has significant personal and religious experiences that contribute to the preacher's personality and pastoral identity. These "organic ingredients" consist of multifarious positive and negative experiences that have left an indelible imprint on the life, identity, and ministry of a preacher. If it is true, as Phillips Brooks once said, that preaching is the communication of truth through personality,[1] then it must follow that the preacher's personality is the sum of vital personal and religious experiences through which preaching comes forth. These organic ingredients are the personal and religious experiences—successes and failures, hopes and disappointments, fortunes and misfortunes—that confront the preacher, unsummoned. These varied and vital experiences constitute the background out of which preaching springs. To be sure, every preacher has a personal story that speaks to the preacher's path to ministry, and to the emotional, intellectual, spiritual, and experiential influences on the preacher's life and ministry. It is without a doubt the preacher's story of God's saving grace amid the vicissitudes and challenges of life.

Surveying Fosdick's life we find that he was by no means an exception to this rule. Such vital experiences for Fosdick—e.g., his brush with death

---

1. Phillips Brooks introduced and explained this phrase in the Lyman Beecher Lectureship on Preaching at the Divinity School of Yale College. See Brooks, *Lectures*, 4–8.

at age three, his intense fear of God's divine wrath at age seven, his crisis of faith at age nineteen while attending Colgate University, his nervous breakdown at twenty-four while attending Union Theological Seminary, and the nervous breakdowns of both his parents—provided the essential substance of his personality and set the trajectory for pastoral ministry. Edmund Holt Linn could not have been more accurate in his analysis of the effect of early personal and religious experiences on the life of the preacher when he argued that such experiences set the pattern for a lifetime of preaching.[2] To get a better understanding of and appreciation for Fosdick's organic ingredients, I now turn to a discussion of some of the important personal and religious experiences that contributed to Fosdick's personality and pastoral identity.

Harry Emerson Fosdick was born in Buffalo, New York, on May 24, 1878, and died in Bronxville, New York, on October 5, 1969. He was born into a family of devout Christians and public-school educators. His paternal grandparents and his father were schoolteachers. His grandfather, John Spencer Fosdick, was a Baptist minister. In addition, his grandmother's father was a Baptist minister as well. John Spencer Fosdick was a schoolteacher in Buffalo for twenty-seven years. Fosdick's father, Frank, taught school for fifty-four years. His mother, Amie, was, as Fosdick tells it, "gay and gracious" but "never physically sturdy and strong."[3] She was an incredible moral force in the life of her children. Although she had a delicate physical constitution, her maternal moral influence was unmistakably robust. She instilled in her children the importance of moral rectitude and irreproachable character.

Fosdick's recollections of early childhood present the picture of a happy, friendly household, though not without challenges. At age five, his twin brother and sister, Raymond and Edith, were born. At age six, young Fosdick was the victim of bullying. When he came whimpering home, his father instructed him to go out and confront the bully and to do his best to "thrash" him. That is exactly what the young Fosdick did, thrashing the

---

2. Linn, *Preaching as Counseling*, 42–43. As regards Fosdick's early religious experiences, Linn keenly observed: "In the case of young Harry Fosdick, his decision to be baptized, his mortal fear of hell, his moments of mystical exaltation, his revolt against orthodoxy and biblical literalism, his slow discovery of an intelligent faith, and a nervous collapse which destroyed his intellectual deceit all combined to lay a groundwork for ministry" (ibid).

3. Fosdick, *Autobiography*, 18.

bully with "unforgettable satisfaction."[4] This incident of self-described bravery is in marked contrast, however, to the way in which Fosdick describes himself elsewhere as a youth: "I was clumsy and ill at ease, unsure of the proper thing to do, embarrassed in conversation, sensitive and self-conscious about my awkwardness, and unhappy at not being able to put my best foot forward."[5] Both statements accurately describe Fosdick's social disposition. We can reconcile this contradiction of social disposition by concluding that Fosdick was a diffident adolescent who displayed occasional bravery. He learned to overcome his social disposition through hard work, self-awareness, and disciplined reading and studying habits.

The influence of Fosdick's parents on his life cannot be overstated. Frank and Amie were deeply Christian and always active in church service. Amie played the piano and Frank the flute. The entire family frequently sang together, since music was for them an important source of therapeutic joy. In addition, the family read books, played games, and discussed important religious and secular matters. The Fosdicks were a happy family, though not without unhappy times. Happiness seemed to come and go in the household. For example, another child was born, Ethel, who died from diphtheria. Understandably, this was a very difficult time for the family. Fosdick recalled that his family feared that he too might succumb to diphtheria. As Fosdick narrates it, his father went through a period of "watching the signs of death creep over me and looking for the end to come before he laid me down."[6] An inadequate income and growing family made life difficult. As if this was not difficult enough, at age seven, Fosdick's mother "collapsed in nervous prostration."[7] As stated earlier, she had a delicate constitution, never quite physically robust. Busied with housekeeping responsibilities, consumed by maternal duties, and worried over financial debt, she suffered a nervous breakdown. This anxiety disorder, sadly enough, haunted the Fosdick household.

Despite these challenges and misfortunes, one of the most significant personal experiences happened to Fosdick at age seven. His pastor, the Reverend Albert Tennant, preached an inspiring sermon on foreign missions. Responding to the sermon, young Fosdick determined to be a Christian. Despite his family's inquiries and protestations ("How could such a young

4. Ibid., 17.
5. Ibid., 42.
6. Ibid., 17.
7. Ibid., 18.

boy know what it means to join the church?" they wondered[8]), Fosdick made a confession of faith and was baptized into the Baptist Church on February 21, 1886. Fosdick's recollections of events from ages eight to eighteen are sketchy at best. Humorously, he related the story of his recitation blunder as a youth at a social event in front of a packed Presbyterian Church. It turns out that after his first recitation, he was awarded with thunderous applause for his superb performance. At his next event, he was humbled in front of a crowded church as he could not get past the second stanza of the poem. Looking back he said that he "ignominiously sat down, and afterward went home to weep bitterly."[9] I surmise that this is why in later years Fosdick devoted such long hours each week to sermon preparation, a point that I will examine in more detail subsequently.

Death and sickness challenged the serenity and stability of the Fosdick home. The young Fosdick experienced the deaths of his aunt Florence and his uncle Albert, which had a profound impact on his life. Fosdick recounts the tragic ordeal quite descriptively: "My mother's sister, Florence, at twenty-eight years of age, died in our home of tuberculosis, and her brother, Albert—thirty years old—returned from a vain search for health in California to die of the same disease four months later. I saw him die. I often wonder that that sight was permitted me, but I recall clearly the pathetic skeleton of that dying man, gasping for breath in his last hour and crying, "Air!"[10] But this was not all. At age ten, Fosdick's father pulled him aside and told him the doctor's prediction that his mother would probably not live another year. Fortunately, she defied the prognosis; she did not die at the predicted time. Fosdick said that he never viewed his mother as an invalid. It is reasonable to conclude that her condition was such that it limited her family responsibilities. Sadly, Fosdick's family struggled with death, sickness, psychological disorders, and financial problems almost constantly.

A democratic family, the Fosdicks convened meetings when important issues or decisions surfaced. Young Fosdick and his twin siblings, Raymond and Edith, were taught to be independent. "Independence," he explained, "was the end and aim of our upbringing—to throw us on our own and enable us to handle ourselves."[11] The fear of letting down their parents was more burdensome than any other kind of childhood discipline.

8. Ibid., 22.
9. Ibid., 30.
10. Ibid., 31.
11. Ibid., 32.

Fosdick's Life and Early Ministry

Religion was the preeminent source of inner turmoil for young Fosdick. Putting the matter forthrightly, Fosdick judged "that from the beginning I was predestined to religion as my predominant interest and major vocation, for from the time I overrode all objections and joined the church when I was seven, I was always struggling with it."[12] He goes on to confess: "But some of the most wretched hours of my boyhood were caused by the pettiness and obscurantism, the miserable legalism and terrifying appeals to fear that were associated with the religion of the churches. It may be that the fear of hell began earlier in my childhood than I now recall."[13] It is quite clear that Fosdick developed a morbid fear of hell, as he recounts in his autobiography: "I was a sensitive boy, deeply religious, and, as I see it now, morbidly conscientious, and the effect upon me of hell-fire-and-brimstone preaching was deplorable. I vividly recall weeping at night for fear of going to hell, with my mystified and baffled mother trying to comfort me."[14] Religious thoughts such as these undoubtedly contributed to Fosdick's repudiation of orthodoxy or traditional religious views.

As a family the Fosdicks enjoyed reading. Indeed, books were one of the most unforgettable aspects of Fosdick's childhood. He developed a love for reading and learning at an early age. In high school, he was introduced to the ancient European classics. He even attempted public speaking, but stage fright initially got the best of him. A shy, embarrassed Fosdick was paralyzed on stage. Elected vice president of the debating society in high school, he was forced into public speaking, and was able to overcome most of his stage fright. The stage fright, "while always present, was not the whole of the experience," he recalled, "for once in a while I got something across and liked it."[15] Fosdick enjoyed being able to connect with his audience. It is difficult to imagine an eminent pastor of a megachurch as a shy, awkward teenager, but that was Harry Emerson Fosdick. His self-descriptive account is telling: "I was clumsy and ill at ease, unsure of the proper thing to do, embarrassed in conversation, sensitive and self-conscious about my awkwardness, and unhappy at not being able to put my best foot forward. Doubtless all youths go through this stage; I suspect that I had more than my share of it."[16] This, too, was Harry Emerson Fosdick.

12. Ibid., 33.
13. Ibid.
14. Ibid., 35–36.
15. Ibid., 42.
16. Ibid.

Life-Situation Preaching for African-Americans

After high school, Fosdick matriculated at Colgate University in Hamilton, New York, where he was introduced to some mind-stimulating personalities. His first year went well for the most part. At the end of the year, though, his father suffered a nervous breakdown, which significantly impacted the family's income. Although he later returned to good health and work, Fosdick was shaken most utterly by this ordeal. A pivotal point of Fosdick's youth occurred when he was nineteen. Burning questions about the faith of his upbringing seared his mind. He concluded that he did not have to believe something simply because it was in the Bible. The final blow to his system of belief in biblical inerrancy came while reading Andrew D. White's two-volume *History of the Warfare of Science with Theology and Christianity*. "Here were the facts," declared Fosdick, "shocking facts about the way the assumed infallibility of the Scriptures had impeded research, deepened and prolonged obscurantism, fed the mania of persecution, and held up the progress of mankind."[17] In response to White's repudiation of fundamentalist views, Fosdick revolted against bibliolatry and theology.

Disrobed of the garment of biblical inerrancy and stripped naked of his religion, Fosdick was much disturbed inwardly and outwardly. His whole life and being were steeped in religion. Accordingly, he wrote: "Religion has been to me the center of my personal life; the church had had my devoted loyalty; and in the family religion had been real and vital. When my religion was disturbed, I was disturbed from the ground up. Others might pass through the phase of questioning and doubt and take it easily. I took it hard."[18] Fosdick grappled seriously with the intellectual credibility of the Christian faith. He pondered whether it was possible to be both intelligent and Christian. Eventually, however, Fosdick's rebellion came full circle, meaning that before long he began questioning his questions, and even doubting his doubts. A return to old orthodox positions was not an option for him. Rather, "seeing the possibility of new positions—old spiritual values in new mental categories" was very attractive.[19] By the end of his senior year at Colgate, Fosdick had decided upon Christian ministry as a vocation. He did not have any interest in denominational affiliation or sectarian Christianity. Nor did he come to definitive conclusions about Christian doctrine. He did know, however, that he wanted to contribute to the spiritual life of his generation.

17. Ibid., 52.
18. Ibid., 53.
19. Ibid., 54.

Fosdick's Life and Early Ministry

After a short stint at Colgate Theological Seminary, Fosdick matriculated at Union Theological Seminary in New York City. He also attended Columbia University, studying theology at Union and philosophy at Columbia. He took a summer job in New York City, working in the Vacation Daily Bible Schools. He worked hard the summer before attending Union, failing to take care of himself physically. In addition to his studies, he helped run the Mission at Mariners' Temple on the Bowery, where he conducted as many as nine meetings in Bowery lodging houses on a single Sunday. The Bowery hosted a notable homeless population, especially Civil War veterans, who migrated to New York in search of occupational prospects. Fosdick's ministry began with the experience of the Bowery, in the slums of the inner city. Indeed this experience was a significant part of his professional development for ministry.

In a very real sense, then, Fosdick's ministry began in New York's underside, "in the raw filth, poverty, and degradation of the Bowery, worse then than is easily imaginable now."[20] Fosdick's biographer, Robert Moats Miller, suggests that the Bowery experience is one of the most causative factors of Fosdick's breakdown. His analysis:

> Nothing in his boyhood or undergraduate years had prepared him for this strange, frightening encounter with New York's underside. Gently nurtured, cherishing Christian ideals and Victorian moral values, knowing only success as a leader in high school and college, easily and always moving his peers with oratory, what a shock for Fosdick to come up against the Bowery citizens. Time and again his exhortations were hooted, his idealistic appeals cynically scorned, his best efforts unavailing. Probably, he was verbally assaulted as a prig; maybe on occasions he felt physically threatened. Many times he might have felt like fleeing or striking back and could not permit himself neither.[21]

The Bowery experience provided Fosdick a first-hand, uncensored exposure to the debauchery of city life. Rare is it that people associate Fosdick's early ministry experience with the slums of New York. But Fosdick did not hesitate to remind readers of his writings that his ministry started in the slums of New York City, not the high society of the posh Riverside Church. Amidst the debauchery and immorality of life in New York City, Fosdick discovered endless opportunities for ministry. City life

---

20. Ibid., 71.
21. Miller, *Fosdick*, 47.

proved to be a breeding ground for fertile ministry. He found ministry to be exhilarating, yet exhausting. His work obligations and academic coursework proved to be too much. Once again tragedy struck. Fosdick, like his mother and father, suffered a nervous breakdown. Recalling that tragic ordeal, he deduced: "I suppose I had a nervous breakdown coming to me. High-strung and sensitive, I was built for one, and the experience was not unfamiliar to my family."[22] Noting the gravity of the matter, he wondered if he really would have cut his throat with a razor if his father had not been there shouting, "Harry! Harry!" It is unclear whether this statement reflects a mental image or an actual event. What is clear, however, is that this experience taught him an invaluable lesson in preparation for ministry. Recollecting that harrowing experience and subsequent self-discovery, he writes:

> In that experience I learned some things about religion that theological seminaries do not teach. I learned to pray, not because I had adequately argued out prayer's rationality, but because I desperately needed help from a Power greater than my own. I learned that God, much more than a theological proposition, is an immediately available Resource; that just as around our bodies is a physical universe from which we draw all our physical energy, so around our spirits is a spiritual Presence in living communion with whom we can find sustaining strength.[23]

As one can see, this event had significant personal and spiritual consequences for Fosdick. God became unquestionably real to him, prayer became absolutely necessary for him, and spirituality awakened within him.[24] This event was indeed one of the most significant experiences in his development and preparation for ministry. He received in-patient psychiatric treatment for four months in The Gleason Sanitarium in Elmira, New York. His full recover, however, took many years and the effects of his breakdown were permanent, as he intimately disclosed: "It took years to surmount the

22. Fosdick, *Autobiography*, 72.
23. Ibid., 75.
24. See Willimon and Lischer, s.v. "Spirituality of the Preacher." Perhaps it is true, as J. Oswald Sanders stated in *Spiritual Leadership*, that "spirituality is not easy to define, but you can tell when it is present" (32). Spirituality is a term with varieties of definitions and expressions. Fosdick's spirituality was evidenced in the way he lived out his "conviction of who he was in relation to God, self, others, and creation" (448–449). His spirituality was centered in how he understood religion, relevant truth, and care and concern for people. He possessed a deep spirituality that was rooted in God and authenticated in his relations with others. To that end, when Fosdick discusses spiritual problems, he is referring to the difficulty of reconciling one's religious convictions with everyday life.

effects of my breakdown and some scars have never left me, but still I can handle the situation now."²⁵ Suggestively, Miller writes: "Fosdick lived with the memory of the nervous breakdowns of both his parents and of his own youthful crack-up, and he lived in fear of a repetition of that nightmare. He had to keep a tight rein. He had to live a careful, ordered existence. Moderation, control, the husbanding of physical energy, the cooling of passions, the calming of excited nerves were essential to his sanity and survival."²⁶ This harrowing experience motivated Fosdick to want to help people face their problems, as he had done.

Fosdick truly believed that this experience gave him insight into his own human nature and that of others. His breakdown and his response to it motivated him to become a devoted student of human nature and psychology. "He possessed," his biographer noted, "an almost spooky seismographic sensitivity to what was troubling the minds and burdening the hearts of the citizens of the twentieth century."²⁷ Fosdick, reflecting many years later, described this event as the most hideous experience of life. In the same way that the nervous breakdown contributed immensely to the development of Fosdick's spiritual life, studies at Union Theological Seminary contributed enormously to the development of his mental faculties. He was able to liberate his mind from fundamentalism without forfeiting his faith. In addition, as a student, Fosdick served as pastor of a rural church during the summer, marking his first "pastoral" experience. He was officially ordained on November 18, 1903. To his delight, his mother attended the ceremony. Unfortunately, this would be the last time he and his mother saw each other. She died from pneumonia in the spring of 1904.

Fosdick's first pastorate was the First Baptist Church of Montclair, New Jersey (1904–1915). Here it was that he had his initial experience with personal counseling, which we will discuss later in more detail. Suffice it say that counseling was central in Fosdick's ministry. At Montclair, he had the freedom to preach sermons laced with modernist observations and sprinkled with positive thinking; he also practiced open communion (open to all believers, not just Baptists). Here, too, he worked hard to find ways

---

25. Fosdick, *Autobiography*, 75. This event had life-changing consequences for Fosdick. In later years he was intentional about taking care of both his mind and his body. In *Autobiography*, Fosdick related that he used his summer resort for the body and winter resort for the mind (117). He also played squash (a ball sport similar to racquetball), tennis, and golf to stay physically active (114).

26. Miller, *Fosdick*, 287.

27. Ibid., 374.

Life-Situation Preaching for African-Americans

to effectively apply the gospel to people's personal and social problems.[28] Because of his emphasis on the people's personal and social problems he was for all intents and purposes a social gospel preacher.

Make no mistake about it, Fosdick's successful preaching ministry came at an exorbitant price. He rented a phoneless room downtown where he secluded himself for four hours every morning to read, study, and write. Fosdick once wrote a letter to his father describing the exacting toll of preaching to expectant crowds. In genuine honesty and humility, he expressed that the growing crowds and the anticipation of facing them every Sunday made him a bit anxious. Concomitant with the gravity with which he approached preaching was semi-overwhelming anxiety. He expressively wrote to his father that: "The crowds continue at the church and I suppose that the anticipation of facing such a mob every Sunday makes the preaching not only exciting but a bit anxious. I do my best not to let the burden of it get through to my nerves but at times I find it difficult to relieve my thoughts, even in hours of relaxation, from the responsibility that the congregation entails."[29] Fosdick, needless to say, took seriously the preaching ministry. The magnitude of the preaching event was not lost on him. Like a prizefighter preparing for a championship bout, Fosdick exercised his intellectual and spiritual muscles daily in preparation for the preaching event. His sermons were the oratory output of disciplined intellectual and spiritual input. He possessed no cheap and easy sermon manufacturing process with which to produce a sermon. It was hard work.

In 1908 Fosdick left Montclair to teach at Union until his retirement in 1946. He was appointed lecturer on Baptist Principles and Polity and instructor in homiletics. In 1915, he became the Morris K. Jessup Professor of Practical Theology. The professorship provided Fosdick the opportunity to travel abroad and preach itinerantly at universities such as Yale and Harvard. There is one other notable event that warrants mentioning in this brief survey of Fosdick's organic ingredients. During World War I (WWI), the Y.M.C.A. extended to Fosdick an opportunity to be an itinerant minister to soldiers in France. He responded with alacrity. Ministry with the soldiers permanently transformed Fosdick's life and understanding of ministry. "No theological course no suburban pastorate, no professorship could have ever taught me what I learned with the troops in wartime," he passionately

---

28. Linn, *Preaching as Counseling*, 42.
29. Miller, *Fosdick*, 98.

observed.[30] Leonora Tubbs Tisdale notes that Fosdick's experience of war and his pastoral care of Soldiers in its midst changed him in a major way. She observed that "when he saw firsthand what war did to people—not only to those civilians who were caught in its crossfire but also to those soldiers that he sent off to battle with a hymn and a prayer, he did a complete about-face."[31] Fosdick lived with and moved among the soldiers, providing ministry as the opportunity arose.[32] Neither he nor his preaching was quite the same after his ministry with the soldiers and what he witnessed. His preaching had a new persuasive power and purpose to it. In his own words: "The effect of my experiences during the war was evident in my preaching. It was much less theological and much more practical than it had been. Not so much apologetics as personal and social ethics became my chief concern."[33] Essentially, preaching to soldiers during combat gave Fosdick an opportunity to experiment with sermons that were practical in nature.[34] Thus Fosdick's preaching became more personal, social, and practical.

Fosdick's insistence upon practicality is what distinguishes his preaching ministry from others. To say that he insisted upon practicality is to say that he believed that the main business of a sermon was the head-on constructive meeting of some problem or real human difficulty that troubled listeners. He was intentional about preaching sermons that addressed such problems, instead of preaching about a biblical text or personality. This is not to say that he did not preach about or from a biblical text—of course he did. He made these things an element of his sermon and not the most important subject thereof. "The preacher's business," Fosdick taught, "is not merely to discuss repentance but to persuade people to repent; not merely to debate the meaning and possibility of Christian faith, but to produce Christian faith in the lives of his listeners; not merely to talk about the available power of God to bring victory over trouble and temptation, but to send people out from their worship on Sunday with victory in their possession."[35]

30. Fosdick, *Autobiography*, 124.
31. Tisdale, *Prophetic Preaching*, 31.
32. Initially a supporter of the war, Fosdick came to vehemently oppose it. Experientially, he saw the effects of the chemical agents of poisonous gas on soldiers, which was a catalyst for his volte-face on war. It was quite easy for him to support the war from a distance, but when confronted face-to-face with the violence and brutality of combat, he could no longer support such a cause.
33. Fosdick, *Autobiography*, 134.
34. Linn, *Preaching as Counseling*, 43.
35. Fosdick, *Autobiography*, 99.

Life-Situation Preaching for African-Americans

This quote best explains and summarizes Fosdick's postwar preaching. As he said often, a preacher's task is to create in his congregation the thing he is talking about. He strongly believed that the sermon's business was to have both a positive and tangible impact on the lives of its listeners. He preached for a verdict, a practical outcome, a tangible difference in the lives of listeners. He held that something ought to take place at the conclusion of a sermon: a decision made, a new way of thinking about a problem, a different way of seeing the world and people, and so on.

In the summer of 1903, while a student at Union Theological Seminary, Fosdick had two pastoral experiences: Guide Board Presbyterian Church of Santa Clara, New York, and the Episcopal Church of the Good Shepard, New York. In the fall of the same year he became an assistant minister to George C. Lorimer, pastor of the Madison Avenue Baptist Church in New York City. On November 18, 1903 Fosdick was ordained in the Madison Avenue Baptist Church. By the time Fosdick graduated from Union Theological Seminary in the spring of 1904 he had some pastoral and preaching experience. Later he would be able to extend his influence beyond the academy and church through his books and radio ministry. He graduated from Colgate University in 1900 and completed his Bachelor of Divinity degree at Union in 1904.

Fosdick served the First Baptist Church of Montclair, New Jersey, for ten years, 1904–14. He was a special preacher in the First Presbyterian Church, New York City, 1919–25, and in 1926 became pastor of the Park Avenue Baptist Church, later the Riverside Church of New York City. He was an instructor and later a professor at Union Theological Seminary for thirty-eight years. His first radio broadcast was in 1926, from the studio of WEAF in New York City. The National Vespers radio program began on October 2, 1927 and ended twenty years later when he retired. His radio ministry was done concurrently with his pulpit ministry. He retired from his professorship and active ministry at the Riverside Church in 1946 at age 67, after twenty years as pastor, and preached his last sermon in 1955 as minister emeritus.[36]

If it is true, as Fosdick posited after his nervous breakdown, that personal experience is the solid ground for assurance, then it must follow that his personal experiences were the solid ground on which he stood and from which he preached. Personal experience was vital in Fosdick's ministry, for the "authority of personal experience was for Fosdick forever

---

36. Coffin, *Union Theological Seminary*, 90.

Fosdick's Life and Early Ministry

to be the primary authority," notes his biographer.[37] Fosdick's disdain for orthodoxy and denominationalism can be traced to various periods of religious turmoil in his life. Similarly, his desire to help people can be traced to personal experiences such as his nervous breakdown and his ministry in France during WWI. His practical approach to preaching can be traced to his first ministry in the slums, his preaching ministry during the first world war, and his frustration with sermon composition during his first pastorates.

In sum, Fosdick's views on life can be traced to the organic ingredients here noted. These ingredients contributed indisputably to Fosdick's personal and pastoral identity. This is not a biographical sketch as such, but rather a chronological account of the prominent personal and religious experiences that helped to form Fosdick's pastoral identity. It is difficult to understand who a preacher is and why a preacher does the things that the preacher does without knowing and understanding the preacher's positive and negative formative experiences. We have seen that Fosdick's early life was fraught with many challenges, setbacks, hiccups, and disappointments. Without a doubt, these events shaped his approach to people, ministry, and preaching. I now turn to a consideration of the factors that prompted Fosdick to jettison the prevailing sermon types of his day, substituting life-situation preaching instead.

New Approach to Preaching

Pastoral ministry can be difficult for young preachers and novice preachers in so-called mainline churches. Observing the ministry of the young white preachers of his day, Fosdick said, "I have seen many a young minister so maltreated by his first parish, so twisted by criticism and disheartened by meanness and coldness, that irreparable damage was done him."[38] Pastoral ministry is not for the faint of heart, to be sure, as it demands the preacher's whole being—body, mind, and soul. The fact is that no part of the tripartite nature—body, mind, and soul—of the preacher remains untouched by ministry. Effective preaching is no less demanding as it requires, if done correctly, rigorous study, disciplined reading habits, intense brainstorming, continuous prayer, and mastery of homiletic approach. The preacher who

---

37. Miller, *Fosdick*, 37.
38. Fosdick, "Learning to Preach," 8. See also Fosdick, *Autobiography*, 87.

Life-Situation Preaching for African-Americans

lacks discipline in these areas will encounter difficulty in composing sermons that are fit for spiritual and intellectual consumption.

Sermon preparation is much like preparation for a surgical procedure in that it demands thoughtful consideration of the patient, duteous care of surgical instruments, respect for written procedures and practices, and the experience and intelligence of a trained medical professional who can address health problems and facilitate healing. Similarly, the preacher must preach with surgical precision, diagnosing and treating the listeners' problems. In the performance of such a vital task, the preacher must weigh the congregation's needs intelligently, reverence the Bible, tradition, and doctrine; and patiently and intelligently meet the vital spiritual needs of the congregation.

Fosdick had a difficult time preparing sermons in his first church, First Baptist Church of Montclair. Sermon preparation proved to be an infinitely frustrating chore. In a telling statement, Fosdick disclosed, "I used to burn the logwood in the morning and the chips at night, and the first sometimes made a slow blaze and the latter a thin one."[39] To make matters worse, his contemporaries' sermons only seemed to exasperate and perplex him further. Fosdick took issue with both the mechanics of their approaches and the way in which they were used. His problem was compounded by the fact that his seminary courses in homiletics proved impracticable, not producing practical results in the lives of listeners. As a student in seminary he listened to informative lectures on preaching that did not have relevance to actual experience. For Fosdick, the teaching of an art such as preaching had to be a practical affair. This is the reason that he, as a professor homiletics at Union Theological Seminary, helped to make the teaching of homiletics a practical affair by requiring each student to preach in chapel to peers and professors, receiving both critique and encouragement. "That kind of training," he wrote longingly, "would have saved me a protracted struggle in my first pastorate, but in those days theologues had little or nothing of such discipline."[40] He concluded that a new approach to preaching was necessary to free him from this homiletical conundrum and pastoral malaise.

Discontented with the prevailing expository and topical sermons of his day, Fosdick experimented with life-situation preaching. He rejected the expository sermon because it proceeded on the assumption that people are interested in the meaning of what a passage means. He dismissed the

---

39. Fosdick, *Autobiography*, 87.
40. Ibid., 83.

topical approach because of its preoccupation with contemporary themes, rather than the concrete problems that people face. He found a middle road between the "doctrinal excesses of expository preaching and the overly secularized strategy of topical preachers."[41] He sought a more effective way to compose meaningful sermons that produced tangible results. Put another way, he sought a practical approach to preaching that would deliver practical results. For Fosdick, the sermon ought to do more than talk about the Bible or a present-day theme; it should bring about transformation of personality; it should do something, prompt a decision or action, in the lives of its listeners. One can only surmise that he would not have lasted long as a preacher if he was forced to continue preaching what he considered ineffective sermons. Nor would he have lasted long if he could not find a different approach to sermon composition.

In Fosdick's view, sermon composition was all the more difficult because the prevailing approaches produced sermons that did not connect with listeners. He viewed such approaches as ineffective and futile. Edmund Holt Linn notes this truth in relation to Fosdick's observation of colleagues in ministry: "Fosdick noticed that there was an appalling number of fed-up, fatigued, bored preachers, to whom preaching had long since become a vexing chore. They had their backs to the wall, constantly under the pressure of 'getting up' weekly sermons, and they struggled desperately to do so."[42] Fosdick's criticism of the preaching methods of his day exposes the weaknesses of their theory and practice. Of course, this is not to say that Fosdick's approach is free of weaknesses, for it most assuredly is not, as is true of all methods.

It is critically important to understand expository and topical preaching independent of Fosdick's critique. What is meant by each of these approaches to preaching? A brief discussion of each follows. The word "exposition" means to bring out what is there. In Latin, the word *exposition* means "setting forth" or making "accessible."[43] The objective of such a sermon is to faithfully bring a message out of Scripture and make that message accessible to contemporary listeners. There are two central principles in expository preaching. First, the authority of Scripture in the pulpit is foremost. That is to say, the preacher's message must be faithful to, consistent with, and authorized by Scripture. The preacher (or expositor) strives to

---

41. See Ryan, *Fosdick*, 11.
42. Linn, *Preaching as Counseling*, 43.
43. Willimon and Lischer, s.v. "Expository Preaching."

understand the biblical text on its own terms through *exegesis*—to interpret a text through analysis of its content—and not *eisegesis*—to interpret the text through pre-conceived ideas of its meanings. Second, the preacher's message must be expressed in clear language and simple logic, accessible to all minds. There are two principle types of expository preaching: verse-by-verse exposition and thematic exposition.

In verse-by-verse expository preaching, the preacher selects a pericope or passage from the Bible and divides it into smaller consumable units of thought, and then proceeds with an exposition of each verse in systematic fashion. Exposition of each verse speaks to a coherent biblical theme or spiritual truth through the interlinking and application of ideas. In thematic expository preaching, the preacher derives the sermon theme from the biblical text but presents that theme in whatever way seems necessary or appropriate to the task of making the message accessible to the listener. The preacher addresses everyday topics by introducing listeners to general themes that appear throughout the Bible, referencing numerous thematic passages in the same preaching event. It is distinguishable from verse-by-verse exposition in that the expositor moves in and out of the biblical text in a manner that is not necessarily verse-by-verse. As is true with every method, expository preaching has strengths and weaknesses. While the strength of expository preaching is that it reinforces the authority and centrality of Scripture in the life of the church, the weaknesses are that it can constrict a preacher's engagement with culture and human experience from the pulpit, and it can lend itself to authoritarianism, resulting in the identification of biblical authority with the preacher's authority, which are completely different.

Fosdick categorized expository sermons as futile and dull. The problem with this method, he reasoned, was that it assumed that people were deeply concerned about what the passage means. Rhetorically, Fosdick inquired into the practical usefulness of the expository sermon, asking: "Who seriously supposes that as a matter of fact, one in a hundred of the congregation cares, to start with, what Moses, Isaiah, Paul, or John meant in those special verses or came to church deeply concerned about it?"[44] Of such a method, he observed: "Only the preacher proceeds still upon the idea that folk come to church desperately anxious to discover what happened to the Jebusites."[45] Fosdick notes that all the great writers of Scripture

---

44. Fosdick, "What Is the Matter With Preaching,?" 30.
45. Ibid.

were interested in and concerned with human living, which, he argued, should be the starting place for modern preachers. This is a point worthy of consideration.

If, as Fosdick maintains, that ancient writers were concerned about life situations during their lifetime, why should modern preachers attempt to grapple with the same issues at the expense of disregarding our contemporary issues? To Fosdick such a question was a moot point, a waste of time. The point of departure for Fosdick was that practical application suffused his sermons, not as material appended to the end thereof. The expository preachers, as he observed them, appended practical or theological application to the end of their sermons. But Fosdick argued that the sermon, from start to finish, was a practical drill. He advised: "Let them not end but start with thinking of the auditors' vital needs, and then let the whole sermon be organized around their constructive endeavors to meet those needs."[46] In a very real sense, Fosdick upended this process; that is, he started with the practical application (the ways in which we should apply the text to our lives) and ended with practical action (the practical steps that we should take in applying this text to our lives).

Whereas the expository sermon is authorized by Scripture and is preached in clear terms, the topical sermon gives a systematic or integrated treatment of a theme considered worthy of discussion. Such a sermon may or may not be biblical. Its key element is its integrative nature. That is, the sermon reaches out in all relevant directions for substance and form to make the best possible case for the matter under consideration. According to the *Encyclopedia of Preaching*, the "problem or issue that gives impetus to a topical sermon may begin at a great distance from the Bible and be led ultimately, almost inevitably, to the scriptures."[47] The *Encyclopedia* notes further that "personal problems of the hearers, controversial issues in the local community, ethical issues of national and international scope, denomination debates, matters of cultural and aesthetic concerns, and congregational challenges—any and all of the fields of inquiry suggest proper topics for preaching."[48] The strength and weakness of the method is that it is the "communication of truth through personality," to use the apposite phrase of Phillips Brooks.[49] The topical sermon has the potential to either

---

46. Ibid., 31.
47. Willimon and Lischer, s.v. "Topical Preaching."
48. Ibid.
49. Brooks, *Lectures*, 4–8.

invoke God's Word for use on a topic or become a discourse on a contemporary issue of importance to the preacher.

The only thing Fosdick deplored more than the expository sermon was the topical sermon. This sermon is predominantly concerned with present-day themes. In an explanation of Fosdick's repudiation of the topical sermon, Robert Moats Miller argues: "Fosdick refused to buy stock in this homiletical bubble, correctly seeing that no man is sufficiently omniscient to speak intelligently on such a wide range of specialized topics and that, above all, worshippers do not come to church to hear opinions on themes that editors, columnists, and radio commentators have been dealing with throughout the week."[50] The topical preacher, observed Fosdick, searches contemporary life in general and the newspaper in particular for subjects. "Instead of starting with a text," explains Fosdick, "they start with their own ideas on some subject of their choice, but their ideas on that subject may be much farther away from a vital interest of the people than a great text from the Bible."[51] Such preachers turned their "pulpits into platforms and their sermons into lectures, straining after some new, intriguing ideas about it."[52]

In Fosdick's estimation, the problem centered on the preacher's method. Indeed, for him, both the expository and topical sermons were organized with the wrong principle in mind. On this score, he argues that: "He [the practitioner of either method] is organizing his sermon around the elucidation of his theme, whereas he should organize it around the endeavor to meet his people's need."[53] He adds: "He is starting with a subject, whereas he should start with an object. His one business is with the real problems of these individual people in his congregation."[54] What mattered most in Fosdick's theory of preaching is the preacher's ability to make real contact with the practical life and daily thinking of listeners.

---

50. Miller, *Fosdick*, 342.
51. Fosdick, "What Is the Matter With Preaching?," 31.
52. Ibid., 32.
53. Ibid.
54. Ibid. In Fosdick's theory of preaching, an object is distinguishable from a subject. He believed that every sermon should have a definite "object" that speaks to a "subject." He sought to get an object for a sermon rather than a subject. The difference, he noted, is that a lecture is chiefly concerned with a subject to be elucidated, whereas a sermon is chiefly concerned with an object to be achieved (99). Linn said that Fosdick thought first about people (objects) and then about ideas (subjects). See Linn, "Techniques of Organization," 186.

Fosdick's Life and Early Ministry

It is important to note that Fosdick did not believe that his approach to preaching diminished the Bible, as is often the claim of life-situation critics, which will be noted subsequently in the discussion on the weaknesses of life-situation preaching. To the contrary, he believed in the Bible's indispensability for contemporary problems. He emphasized this point: "I had been suckled on the Bible, knew it and loved it, and I could not deal with any crucial problem in thought and life without seeing text after text lift up its hands begging to be used."[55] The Bible was for him the sourcebook for answers to the people's problems. Consequently, Fosdick did not have an issue with the Bible per se, but with the way in which the Bible was being used in preaching. The status quo of selecting "texts from the Bible and then proceed[ing] to give their historic setting, their logical meaning in the context, their place in the theology of the writer, with a few practical reflections appended"[56] was neither attractive nor practical to him. In simple terms, Fosdick liked using the Bible, but not in the same way that many of his contemporaries did.

In advocating Fosdick's life-situation preaching, Linn asserts: "The writers of the Bible themselves were interested in such human problems as unbelief, perplexity, sin, and desire, and the preacher honors them by starting, as they did, with some such real need."[57] For Linn, the expository method, for the preacher of a life-situation sermon "is a gross misuse of the Bible."[58] Fosdick believed that the Bible was an "amazing compendium of experiments in human life under all sorts of conditions,"[59] and he used the Bible practically, relevantly, and intelligently to address the contemporary problems of his day. Eugene May maintains that Fosdick did not use the Bible merely to justify his own ideas or as an apologist, but rather to relate its truths to contemporary moral and spiritual issues. In his analysis of Fosdick's use of the Bible, May maintained: "He holds that some of the Bible simply is not relevant to life today and some is outgrown by moral and spiritual progress; but, when he uses it, one has the sense that he is using it fairly and according to the best interpretation possible."[60] To clarify, Fosdick used the Bible resourcefully and practically, although he did not see

---

55. Fosdick, *Autobiography*, 95.
56. Fosdick, "What Is the Matter With Preaching?," 30.
57. Linn, *Preaching as Counseling*, 54.
58. Ibid.
59. Fosdick, "What Is the Matter With Preaching?," 30.
60. May, "Bible in Preaching," 83.

the relevance of some of its material. Using the Bible intelligently, for Fosdick, was not the same as believing something or everything in the Bible. One could use the Bible intelligently without subscribing to the unscientific claims like biblical miracles; such claims, he surmised, were incompatible with modern science.

The fact of the matter is, Fosdick used the Bible differently from his contemporaries because his aim was different. That is, he aimed at practical results. Critics of life-situation preaching tend to question its merits because the approach, as they see it, diminishes the importance of the Bible. The matter of Fosdick's use of the Bible in preaching will be discussed later. Expending time on this topic is important for the argument of this book. For Fosdick, these approaches did not meet his pastoral objective of ministering to peoples' contemporary problems and needs. Having presented the factors that motivated Fosdick to experiment with a different approach to preaching, it is now time to examine his preference for life-situation preaching, the subject of chapter two.

2

The Nature of Life-Situation Preaching

Preaching People's Needs

As discussed in the previous chapter, Fosdick had an urgent need for a new approach to preaching. He desired an approach that took seriously people's personal, social, and spiritual problems. He was not concerned with obscure biblical texts or, as he saw it, outmoded orthodox doctrine. Disenchanted with the prevailing homiletics of his day and discouraged by what he saw as an ineffective preparation-of-sermon process for which his courses in homiletics had done little to correct, Fosdick tried his hand at life-situation preaching. To date, he is considered the master of this type of preaching. While it is true that no other preacher has done as much as Fosdick to influence and promote this approach to preaching, it is also true that this approach both predates and postdates Fosdick.

In his published dissertation on Fosdick, Harry Black Beverly Jr. discovered that Henry Ward Beecher, Albert Edward Day, Walter Russel Bower, Charles S. Horne, Wm. J. Tucker, Ch. D. Williams, Charles E. Jefferson, John Brown, and Phillips Brooks all discussed life-situation preaching in their respective Lyman Beecher Lectures on Preaching at Yale University.[1] Consequently, Fosdick was neither the sole advocate nor the sole practitioner of this approach. Although life-situation preaching is not as popular as it was once, it is still used in preaching circles. It is truly unfortunate,

1. Beverly, Jr., *Fosdick's Predigtweise*, 17.

Life-Situation Preaching for African-Americans

though, that this approach to preaching is not mentioned or taught in divinity schools and seminaries where preaching is a part of the curriculum. Preaching, as is true of many things in the twenty-first century, has become a subjective enterprise; preachers exercising their gift in a way that is pleasing to them.[2] That's fine and dandy, but is the chosen approach effective?

Contemporary preachers face difficulty when trying to answer definitional questions about life-situation preaching such as what is life-situation preaching, and is it considered a type of preaching? Why do authors of histories on preaching, encyclopedias on preaching, and introductory works on preaching intentionally omit life-situation preaching? There is, to be sure, a paucity of literature on the subject. The fact is, life-situation preaching has never held the same status as other types of preaching. Preachers and homileticians alike view life-situation preaching with suspicion, if not condescension, because of the absence of theological substance in its contents. Life-situation preaching, they say, is grounded in positive thinking and not the power of the gospel. Then again, is it not human nature to disregard or deny the importance of things that are at variance with our own tradition or perspective on society and the world? Even the most astute homileticians have homiletical blind spots that prevent them from seeing the value of preaching theories and approaches to preaching (e.g., African-American preaching) at variance with their own tradition, standard, or theory of preaching. In any event, life-situation preaching has many features that make it a sound approach to preaching. First, it is the essence of the ministry of Jesus. Second, it is a practical approach to preaching. Third, it is concerned with listeners' vital needs. Fourth, it is *situationally-enlightened* preaching. Finally, it is *solution-oriented* preaching.

Describing the ministry of Jesus, Fosdick emphasized that "the Master, far from being interested only in men's souls, was immensely concerned about their day-by-day, practical, mundane needs."[3] This principle is critical to Fosdick's life-situation preaching. He stressed further that Jesus' final test at judgment was whether he had met the practical needs of the poor and dispossessed, that is, "fed the hungry, given drink to the thirsty, and

---

2. Questions regarding what constitutes a "standard"—individuality/conformity, subjectivity/objectivity, tradition/innovation, and so on—are raised anew with each generation. Ours is no exception. With this in mind, no one can refer to any particular standard as "the" standard, for approaches to preaching are subject to ecclesial, social, and contextual forces that have a say in the preacher's approach.

3. Fosdick, *Great Time to Be Alive*, 21.

The Nature of Life-Situation Preaching

clothed the naked."[4] Life-situation preaching, especially in Fosdick's case, is concerned with such practical aspects of everyday life. "Everywhere in the Gospel," explains Fosdick, "Jesus is presented as wanting us to have what we naturally want to have—physical well-being, economic security, food, clothes, health."[5]

In his analysis of life-situation preaching, Harold Ruopp wrote that life-situation preaching is an approach to preaching and not necessarily a method or type of preaching (for example: textual, expository, or topical).[6] Regardless of what we call it, life-situation preaching has had, and will have, a presence and audience in Christian ministry. If life-situation preaching lacks a definition, let a description suffice. By way of description, life-situation preaching is an approach to preaching that starts with people's social, personal, and spiritual problems and attempts to bring the Bible and relevant truths to bear on such problems in order to prompt a decision or decisive action from the listener. Describing the approach of the life-situation preacher, Ruopp explains: "In this approach the preacher begins not with his own subjective interests and desires nor even necessarily with a text, but with some concretized question, problem, difficulty or 'life situation' which people are facing (whether they can always articulate it clearly or not) and then with that situation constantly in mind he works in the direction of a 'solution' of the problem, a solution which will help them face life more steadily, realistically, creatively, courageously, and redemptively."[7]

The life-situation preacher is helping people to understand life more deeply. To that end, insight into human nature is critical. The reader does well to understand life-situation preaching as *an* approach to preaching and not necessarily a method that demands pulpit fidelity. Preachers are unique. Congregations are unique. Problems are unique to individual personalities. The dynamics of these things may be such that this approach is ineffective in meeting their congregation's real needs, and, as a result, a different approach may be warranted. Life-situation preaching does not presume that everyone who comes to church has major problems, that the church is saturated with nothing but people who have difficult problems. Nor does it presume that the life-situation preacher has all the answers to humanity's profound universal problems. It does presume, though, that

4. Ibid.
5. Ibid.
6. Ruopp, "Life Situation Preaching," 116.
7. Ibid.

Life-Situation Preaching for African-Americans

preaching at its best should respond thoughtfully and practically to the voiced and unvoiced concerns of the congregation; it should connect with vital human needs and interests.

In his treatment of life-situation preaching, Charles Kemp teaches that this approach rests on the supposition that there are people in the church who are in need of the preacher's practical understanding of their needs and how to meet them homiletically. Kemp cautions that this does not mean that every listener who comes to church has a major problem or find life burdensome. Far from it!, he argues. In his view, the supposition in life-situation preaching speaks to the reality "that there is probably no congregation in America, of any size whatever, that does not include some people who are in need of real help."[8] Kemp's point is that there are people sitting in the pews who are in desperate need of answers to their perplexing questions and major problems. To fully understand and respond to the people's needs, the perceptive preacher understands that no problem concerns an individual more than his or her own problem; and that the preacher's task is to respond accordingly with incisive and decisive preaching. The expectation, then, is that something relevant will be said from the pulpit that will help people live more faithfully and tenaciously in the face of their problems.

Edgar N. Jackson, a student of Fosdick, takes up the case of human needs and what is implied in preaching to meet such needs. Jackson maintains that the ministry of Jesus provides the quintessential example of life-situation preaching, noting, as did Fosdick, the life-situational element in Jesus' ministry. The example of Jesus provides "certain requisite presuppositions for preaching as a form of group soul-healing."[9] The ministry of Jesus, he adds, was a ministry that gave people courage to face their weaknesses, to understand their situations, to show love and concern for others, and the opportunity for growth in their understanding of and relationship with God. Along the same lines, Jackson maintains that there have always been the recognition of problems and the possibility of solutions, with the emphasis on helping the individual to face the future in contrast to condemning past behavior. Analyzing the ministry of Jesus further, Jackson was convinced that "at the core of the ministry of Jesus was a sense of

---

8. Kemp, *Life-Situation Preaching*, 13.
9. Jackson, *Preach People's Needs*, 12.

The Nature of Life-Situation Preaching

concern, even compassion, that made the individual in the group feel that there was a friend to be trusted and followed."[10]

Fosdick's influence on Jackson is clearly seen when he goes on to argue that "preaching to human needs demands the ability to visualize the congregation, even while the sermon is being prepared."[11] That is to say, a critical part of sermon composition is the visualization of those to whom the sermon is directed. Preachers should not only recall faces within the congregation, they must be attuned to the vital concerns and problems that afflict such faces. The life-situation preacher should be conscious of the spiritual needs of the people and capable of meeting such needs through the medium of preaching. Such a preacher must "speak from a soul that knows the meaning and power of God's healing love."[12] Jackson notes that Harold Ruopp once compiled data taken from a survey of congregants' needs, which speaks tellingly to the indispensability of the life-situation approach to preaching. Citing Ruopp's data, Jackson notes:

> In response to specific questions nearly four thousand replies indicated that about half of the persons felt the major problems of their lives to be such personal matters as futility, insecurity, loneliness, marriage problems, sex, alcoholism, false ideas of religion and morals, inferiority, suffering, illness, frustrations, and guilt feelings. Nearly a quarter of the persons were concerned about family problems, child training, infidelity, separation, divorce, poor adjustment to marriage, religious differences in the home, and other problems that are symptoms of personal problems as they touch the lives of others. The remaining fraction were concerned with social community, and national problems, or the more traditional religious concerns.[13]

The preacher who is able to identify such needs and see people in terms of such needs has taken a very important step toward *situationally-enlightened* preaching that gets at the heart of people's problems. Jackson cautions against unrealistic expectations when preaching to people's needs, as such preaching can exacerbate matters. To this point, he argues that a sermon can miss the homiletical mark by setting false goals, stimulating unhealthy resentments, promising a security that is unreal, encouraging

10. Ibid., 12–13.
11. Ibid., 13.
12. Ibid.
13. Ibid., 14.

either of opposite extremes (submissiveness, on the one hand, or aggressiveness, on the other) that could result in more acute personality difficulties.[14] To this end, a life-situation sermon "should face the reality of life honestly, proceed creatively toward goals that are reasonable and challenging to the best in life."[15] In the final analysis, the aim of the life-situation sermon is to meet life-disrupting forces with practical instruction founded on biblical truths. It is one thing to instruct a hungry person to catch a fish for food, it is quite another to tell a hungry person how to acquire the tools and bait with which to fish and where to find adequate fish, all based on sound fishing practices.

Robert J. McCracken succeeded Fosdick as pastor at Riverside Church. During McCracken's installation service, Fosdick gave him a formidable charge, conveying the church's expectation for excellence in preaching:

> Welcome to this church. It is a seven-day-week affair with more things going on here than you can possibly keep track of. Don't try to. Most of all we want your message in the pulpit, born out of long hours of study, meditation, and prayer. Guard your morning privacy as a sacred trust! We have called you because you are a great Christian with a message for this generation. That you will wisely counsel with us in practical affairs, and be endlessly helpful in personal consultations, we take for granted. But what most of all we want from you is that on Sunday morning you should come into this pulpit here like Moses with the word of God emerging from his communion on the mountain, who wist [sic] not that his face shone.[16]

Although McCracken's comments on life-situation preaching have been sparse, what he did say adds value to our discussion. Prior to Riverside, he practiced expository preaching, moving from biblical exposition to theological analysis to practical application. (It is worth acknowledging that Fosdick and McCracken had African-American counterparts, e.g., Vernon N. Johns, James H. Robinson, and John Malcus Ellison, who were also life-situation preachers.) Soon enough McCracken jettisoned expository preaching for life-situation preaching. He, like his predecessor

---

14. Ibid., 15.

15. Ibid.

16. Fosdick's charge was printed in the *New York Herald Tribune*, October 3, 1945; see also Miller, *Fosdick*, 334.

The Nature of Life-Situation Preaching

Fosdick, favored an approach to preaching that connected with listeners' vital needs and interests.

In *The Making of the Sermon*, McCracken points out that the point of departure for the life-situation preacher is a live issue of some kind; personal, social, ethical, or theological. Preachers must make it their business, he advised, "to get at the core of the problem, and, that done, he goes on to work out the solution, with the biblical revelation, and the mind and spirit of Christ, as the constant points of reference and direction."[17] In a very real sense, then, life-situation preaching is not only *situationally-enlightened* preaching, it is also *solution-oriented* preaching. It speaks to the core of what is ailing the listener. McCracken instructed preachers to "start your sermon by sketching the problem," which is "practical, living, urgent."[18] The problem is where people need help, he says. Even if the problem is not relevant to a particular listener, the listener will feel the impact of the words on his neighbors. The urgent need today, he stressed, is to bring preaching close to life, regardless of one's homiletic approach. For McCracken, this was the need of listeners and the task of the sermon. He concludes: "Yes, whether expository, ethical, devotional, theological, apologetical, social, psychological, evangelical, topical, bring preaching close to life."[19] The point here is that one's method or approach to the preparation and delivery of a sermon is subordinate to meeting the urgent needs of listeners by bringing biblical revelation and practical counsel to bear on their problems.

In *Building Sermons to Meet People's Needs*, Harold T. Bryson and James C. Taylor posit that a sermon will be people oriented when the preacher thinks about the various needs of the people. The preacher assesses and addresses the needs of the community, in each person's particular situation, with the word of God. Understanding the community's needs, they argue, heightens the preacher's sense of building and delivering sermons to meet human needs. Critical to meeting such needs is a basic understanding of human needs and human behavior. Bryson and Taylor addressed the importance of the preacher's comprehension of Abraham Maslow's seven different categories of human need: aesthetic; knowing and understanding; self-actualization; esteem; love, affection, belonging; safety; and physiological. Understanding Maslow's concept of hierarchy of needs, they propound, will provide the preacher with insight into human needs. Perceptively, they

17. McCracken, *Sermons*, 62.
18. Ibid., 63.
19. Ibid.

Life-Situation Preaching for African-Americans

note: "Until these basic needs are met in a reliable, continuing manner, a person's life will be dominated by them. He will not be interested deeply in other things while this domination lasts."[20] Therefore, it is important that the preacher is able to discern people's personal problems with insights from Maslow's concept.

People come to worship with all kinds of problems—financial distress, broken relationships, pressing deadlines, and unmet spiritual and physical needs, and other factors—for which they are seeking answers. Preaching at its best, according to life-situation proponents, speaks to these unmet needs with the power of the gospel. Now, it should be noted that not all life-situation preaching suggests that the starting place for the sermon is human needs or people's problems. Bryson and Taylor maintain that the building and delivery of a sermon has both a human and dynamic element. They admonish preachers to "resolve to study carefully the Bible so that the foundation for your sermons will be a word from God rather than a human opinion."[21] They use the analogy of a builder to help the preacher understand that the quality of a building, i.e., the sermon, is going to be determined by the character and skill of the builder. "If you were going to build a house," they reason, "the quality of the house would be determined greatly by the character and skill of the builder. You need to think of yourself as a builder of sermons to meet people's needs."[22] For Bryson and Taylor, the foundation of any sermon should be the gospel of Jesus Christ.

The preacher should be skilled in the tools of the preacher's trade—biblical exegesis, audience analysis, congregational context, and the creative use of experience and Scripture, to name a few—so as to bring her skills, knowledge, and experience to bear on contemporary life situations. Without such skills, the preacher's product, the sermon, is going to be substandard, ineffective, not producing practical results in listeners' lives. This is not to say unqualifiedly that there are no preachers who have produced quality sermons without having access to and adequate use of such tools. Certainly not! Many are they who have mastered the art of preaching through imitation of well-known preachers or through self-study. Although few and far between, there are autodidacts who have achieved excellence in preaching,

---

20. Bryson and Taylor, *Sermons*, 44. Life-situation preaching so discussed removes the barrier separating this approach to preaching from African-American preaching. We will take up this matter shortly in our discussion of the similarities between the two.

21. Ibid., 13.

22. Ibid., 15.

The Nature of Life-Situation Preaching

as is true of art, poetry, music, and the like,. At any rate, the point here is that the preacher as a builder of sermons must possess knowledge of God's word in order to compose sermons that will truly meet people's needs; and the preacher must understand people's life situations so that the gospel can be brought to bear on human needs and problems.

It is as important for preachers to know and understand what is happening in the lives of their people as it is for them to know and understand the Bible. Preachers who lack insight into human nature can benefit from pastoral counseling. Insight into people's problems does not come through osmosis, education alone, or divine revelation, at least not for most of us. It comes through experiential and vital contact with people. Fosdick believed that preaching and pastoral counseling were one inseparable function of the preacher. In fact, he put pastoral counseling foremost in his ministry. In the next section, I examine the relationship between Fosdick's life-situation preaching and pastoral counseling.

Life-Situation Preaching and Pastoral Counseling

Young preachers and novice preachers can benefit from life-situation preaching, although the lack of life experiences and maturity often times presents a problem for many such preachers. "Personal counseling," Fosdick believed, "does not begin full force in the experience of a young minister fresh from seminary."[23] According to Fosdick's logic, the problem is that young preachers are too inexperienced and immature, which prevents older adults from seeking the young preacher's advice. In 1952, Fosdick published an article in *Pastoral Psychology* entitled "Personal Counseling and Preaching."[24] This article represents his most definitive remarks on the two disciplines. Here Fosdick discusses the relationship between personal counseling and preaching.

Fosdick believed that preaching and pastoral counseling were not two distinct functions, but one inseparable function of the preacher—two "indispensable offices of one vocational task"; inseparably conjoined in one office.[25] In fact, Fosdick often said that he approached the pulpit as though

---

23. Fosdick, *Autobiography*, 93.

24. Fosdick, "Personal Counseling and Preaching."

25. Miller, *Fosdick*, 346. In *Life-Situation Preaching*, Kemp wisely advises that: "It is not a question of which is the more important, preaching or pastoral work; both must be done well" (20). Fosdick poured his heart into each of these pastoral functions to reach

Life-Situation Preaching for African-Americans

he was beginning a personal consultation.[26] Personal counseling helps the preacher to develop effective sermons that address listeners' vital needs. Fosdick was convinced that personal counseling is as beneficial to preaching as preaching is to personal counseling.[27] The hours spent in personal counseling provide deep insight into human nature that translates into relevant content for preaching. He said that the "right kind of preacher is coerced to become a personal counselor, and the right kind of personal counselor gains some of the most necessary ingredients of preaching."[28]

For Fosdick, personal counseling is central to Christian ministry, and he reminded his listeners (public ministry) and readers (literary ministry) of this fact: "I am commonly thought of as a preacher, but I should not put preaching central in my ministry. Personal counseling has been central. My preaching at its best has itself been personal counseling on a group scale."[29] This should not be underestimated or understated. The centrality of personal counseling in Fosdick's ministry is important because everything he did in ministry, with an audience or individual, centered on the dignity and worth of the individual. His preaching, although addressed to a group, was a direct address to the individual within the group. The effect of such an approach is that the individual within the congregation feels as though the preacher is talking directly to him or her. It was not uncommon to hear a listener express gratitude for the individual directness of Fosdick's preaching. Though seated in the crowd, one such listener reflected: "Dr. Fosdick always made me feel as though he had prepared that particular sermon especially for me. Never before, and never since, have I heard sermons that 'got to me' the way Dr. Fosdick's sermons did."[30] The church needs such preaching. We need sermons that "get to people" the way Fosdick's did.

---

people on a practical level.

26. Fosdick, "Personal Counseling and Preaching," 55. This is evidence of Fosdick's personalism. He was familiar with the work of the personalist, Borden Parker Bowne, the Boston University personalist and "father of American personalism." Fosdick notes in *Autobiography* that early in his ministry he was strongly attracted to Bowne's personalism (64).

27. "Personal counseling" and "pastoral counseling" are used interchangeably throughout this book. Fosdick referred to the pastoral function of counseling as "personal counseling."

28. Fosdick, *Autobiography*, 51.

29. Ibid., 215.

30. Miller, *Fosdick*, 97.

The Nature of Life-Situation Preaching

Fosdick's hortative counseling regarding the importance of personal counseling for the preaching ministry is worthy of consideration. What is ultimately at stake is the decentralization of the individual. Individuals, not preaching, should be central in ministry, according to Fosdick, who constantly admonished his staff at Riverside to focus on the individual. Emphasizing this cardinal principle, Fosdick directed his staff to concentrate on the individuals within the crowds, for "nothing in the long run matters in this church except what happens to them."[31] The relationship of personal counseling to preaching is that each function informs and enhances the other. The pulpit and the counseling room are both places in which help-seekers find help for their problems. Both activities center on the individual. Fosdick explained that the creative center of his ministry was the firsthand dealing with individuals, which in turn provided a fruitful source of his preaching.[32] There are a few things to ponder when considering the effect of personal counseling on preaching.

First, in the personal consultation room, the preacher is confronted with myriad issues and concerns, which provides insight into listeners' lives. "Personal counseling imparts to the preacher a practical familiarity with human structure which he would not otherwise obtain," according to Linn.[33] As a result, ever once and again a real problem is presented and is solved with the power of the gospel. Fosdick affirmed as much in his experiences with personal counseling: "The Gospel works. One sees a miracle take place before one's eyes. A life is made over, a family is saved, a valuable youth turns about in his tracks and heads right, a potential suicide becomes a happy and useful member of society..."[34] Such experiences are the results of effective pastoral counseling. Second, personal counseling deepens the preacher's confidence in the gospel. Watching the transformation of human personality through the gospel breeds hope and faith in the preacher and listener alike. Such an experience can propel the preacher into the pulpit with mountain-moving, results-producing sermons. Third, personal counseling tends to shift the preacher's mind from an obsession with his sermon's subject to a purposeful concern about its listeners. In Fosdick's theory of preaching, the sermon should not be a harmless discussion on a subject. On the contrary, as noted previously, it should have a definite

---

31. Fosdick, *Autobiography*, 212.
32. Ibid., 218.
33. Linn, *Preaching as Counseling*, 24.
34. Ibid., 52.

objective, a purpose. Fosdick offers a point of clarification: "We are not saying that personal counseling by itself can make a good preacher. Obviously it cannot. But it can give tone and direction and significance to preaching which our generation critically needs."[35] Here Fosdick makes clear that personal counseling helps a preacher preach sermons that address the practical concerns of listeners, not help preachers to be "good preachers."

Fosdick counseled and preached to real people with real problems. He did so "using whatever biblical, topical, illustrative material could be marshaled to accomplish the transformation of persons."[36] "Such sermons," Linn observed, "suggest rather than command, explain rather than exhort, and discuss rather than dictate."[37] The point here is that personal consultation and preaching have an interdependent relationship in which one informs and contributes to the other, making it possible to intelligently bring the gospel to bear on people's real problems in a practical, person-centered way. Fosdick was an exceptional life-situation preacher and counselor. For Fosdick, the consultation room was a laboratory in which to study and experiment with human nature in order to treat the maladies of his day. The advantages of personal counseling were so apparent to Fosdick's ministry that he identifies pastoral counseling as the mainstay of his lengthy ministry, as we have noted. It should be pointed out, however, that Fosdick went as far as to claim that he never could have preached for twenty years without the creative experience of personal counseling.[38]

Most contemporary preachers and homileticians alike understand the importance of preaching sermons that are close to life. Although they do not discuss life-situation preaching as an approach to preaching, they do, however, understand and stress the importance of preaching to life situations, as knowing and understanding the existential life situations of listeners is critical to any homiletical method or approach. Yes, Fosdick used therapeutic and psychological techniques to enhance his preaching, but this

---

35. Fosdick, "Personal Counseling and Preaching," 53–54.

36. Linn, *Preaching as Counseling*, 25.

37. Ibid.

38. It is not difficult to see why this approach was appealing to Fosdick. Many people who are in the counseling field are people who have had a nervous breakdown or some other psychological or counseling-related problem themselves. After his breakdown, Fosdick disclosed that he wholeheartedly wanted to help ordinary people get through their problems. To this end, he wrote: "One effect of it [nervous breakdown] on me was to make me want to get at folks—ordinary, everyday folks—and try to help them" (*Autobiography*, 78).

does not diminish the effectiveness of his method. Remember, his method was designed to meet the felt needs of his audience and produce within them the subject matter of the sermon—joy or self-love, for example. Now that we have explored the benefits of personal counseling to preaching and vice versa, I want to take up the matter of the indistinguishable qualities of life-situation preaching and African-American preaching.

Life-Situation Preaching and African-American Preaching

In 1911 Fosdick was made Associate Professor of Homiletics at Union Theological Seminary. One of the requirements was a preaching assignment in which students preached a prepared sermon to classmates and the professor. William A. Spurrier recollected that there was a black student in class who possessed the necessary qualities of a preacher. Reminisced he, "There was a black student in this . . . class who had near-perfect diction, a marvelous speaking voice, and was obviously an educated and fairly sophisticated person—just like the rest of us white fellows thought we were. So the black delivers this sermon in a most polished and careful style, modulated and refined, cultivated and clear—beautiful—so we all thought. Fosdick's critique was as follows: 'Mr. _____, your sermon was excellent in substance reflecting the heart of the Gospel. As for your delivery: it was clear, concise, orderly and exceedingly well-tailored. But where was your passion, man? Don't you believe what you preached? Have you no feelings? Surely, one of the great talents of your people is your history of suffering, hope, despair. You can understand the Gospel better than we because of what we have done to you. So do not imitate our refined clarity; let go with your spiritual passion, man, let go and let us have it.'"[39] It seems that Fosdick confused passion with belief, especially in the context of preaching, but the point here is that the harsh experiences of African-Americans, which are involuntarily and ineradicably stored on their mental hard drives, give them an extensive database from which to pull vital information that help them relate to and communicate with eager listeners. Truth to tell, Fosdick was well aware of the creative capacity of African-Americans to bring the truth of the gospel to bear on social ills, as is demonstrated by his homiletical critique of the black student.

39. Quoted in Miller, *Fosdick*, 324.

Life-Situation Preaching for African-Americans

Although Fosdick did not develop his approach to preaching in such a way that it took into consideration or spoke to the unique conditions of African-Americans, he understood nevertheless that their lived social experiences in America contributed to their understanding of society and their worldview, especially as it relates to the preacher's ability to preach passionately and convincingly. It is of vital importance to point out that Fosdick understood the emotional context of the African-American worship service and the celebratory element of the African-American sermon, not to suggest that the African-American preaching tradition or worship service is homogeneous. Effusive praise, emotive content, demonstrative affection, and celebratory conclusion are integral parts of the African-American preaching and worship experience to be sure. Ultimately, the preacher is concerned to gladden hearts, unburden consciences, uplift broken spirits, and effect salvation with the power of the gospel. What some characterize as emotional bosh is for the black churchgoer spiritual, emotional, and mental catharsis of repressed emotions. Social, economic, and political oppression engenders headaches and heartaches. Nothing is more uplifting and gratifying to the oppressed and downtrodden than to be propped up with the sustaining power of the gospel. Even more gratifying and uplifting is the belief that God is clairaudient in that God hears the inaudible cry of the poor and dispossessed. A sermon that appeals solely to the cognitive faculty with no consideration for the emotive or intuitive is devoid of something vital.

In *They Like to Never Quit Praisin' God: The Role of Celebration in Preaching*, Frank A. Thomas, who will be discussed presently, analyzes the emotional context and process in African-American preaching. Thomas holds that the nature and purpose of African-American preaching is to help people experience the assurance of grace that is the gospel of Jesus the Christ.[40] "Celebratory design" is the name Thomas gives to African-American preaching that celebrates the assurance of grace in people's lives. Highlighting the emotional context in which communication takes place, he notes that human communication consists of various emotions. Therefore, it behooves the preacher to consider this often-neglected contextual phenomenon when preaching. The Euro-American homiletic tradition has ignored the emotional context and process, observes Thomas, and focused on cerebral process and words. The deductive rationalistic approach with its elucidation of a proposition is no longer in vogue because its goal was

---

40. Thomas, *Never Quit Praisin' God*, 3.

The Nature of Life-Situation Preaching

merely to impart information or give instruction, mindless of the emotional context and process. For Thomas, the key to moving beyond the limitations of the cerebral process is to incorporate five essential elements into the sermon: dialogical language, knowledge of core belief (cognitive, emotive, and the intuitive), concern for emotive movement, unity of form and substance, and creative use of reversals (paradox). What we observed in Fosdick's critique of the black student's preaching was that the celebratory element and intense passion—characteristic of some African-American preaching—was noticeably absent.

However trained or skilled in preaching, the preacher's cultural, economic, political, and social sensibilities inform the preacher's interpretation and presentation of the gospel. Fosdick's sermons are directed at upper and upper-middle class churchgoers, and they reflect the rural, upper New York environment in which he lived. Observed his biographer, "His sermons are informed by a pastoral and bucolic sensibility, not by an urban one. They smell of the orchards of upper New York, the heather of Scotland, the pines of Maine, the mountain air of Switzerland, the fresh waters of Lake Chautauqua, and the salty ocean surrounding Mouse Island."[41] If it is true that these elements informed his sermons, it must logically follow that these elements also limited his sermons. Note, too, that the elements that make for good preaching in one context may not work equally well in another. Nothing in Fosdick's upbringing suggests that he encountered the life-limiting, life-extracting experiences—oppression, scorn, stigmatization, ostracization, racism, brutality, and psychological abuse—that African-Americans face daily.

Spurrier's recollection reveals Fosdick's appreciation for the preaching ability of African-Americans, which is forged and perfected in the crucible of challenging life situations. This is not to be taken lightly. Fosdick's preaching at its best could never replicate the urgent and perfervid fierceness of civil rights leaders and protesters who had been beaten with a police baton, fisted by rabid racists, sprayed with the stinging blast of a high-pressure water hose, and shredded by the meat-grinding bite of a police canine. Such a preacher limps into the pulpit with extraordinary fortitude and fierceness unavailable to those who have not been baptized into the cold river of human suffering. The incomprehensible depth of such experiences informs and influences preaching in ways that the uninitiated appreciate but are unable to recreate. Thus, life-situation preaching for African-Americans

41. Miller, *Fosdick*, 352.

extends beyond the circumscribed limits of Fosdick's preaching practices in that it takes seriously and is sensitive to the historical and existential experiences of African-Americans.

In *Preaching with Sacred Fire*, the editors consider three principles of black preaching: (1) the centrality of the Bible, (2) picture painting and narration of the Bible, and (3) a close observation of life known as existential exegesis.[42] Regarding the third principle, one editor notes that the African-American preacher desires relevance and that the preacher's sermons will "help the hearer at points of need, not just reach them as abstract doctrine."[43] In addition to the three principles noted, the editors note four classifications of homiletics: *social activist preaching*, which provides the spiritual, moral, and cultural underpinnings for liberation struggles; *black identity preaching*, which seeks to reconstruct blacks' humanity, dignity, and self-esteem; *cultural survival preaching*, which constructs and maintains black culture; and *empowerment preaching*, which provides an unequivocal message of wealth and success through change in consciousness as a liberation strategy.[44] Each of these classifications concerns existential life situations, such as intracommunity violence and police brutality against African-Americans, which will be discussed in chapter 6.

White preaching in mainline churches is different from black preaching. It is no small compliment when the late David Buttrick, a distinguished white homiletics professor at the Divinity School at Vanderbilt University, said that since 1960 the best preaching in America has been happening in African-American settings, and that, as a teacher in both black and predominately white theological schools, "African-American students generally know more Bible than white students, often by heart."[45] Buttrick observes two things about black preaching that are worth mentioning. First, he says that black preaching observes the Bible as story, not as a written-down book. Black preaching, says Buttrick, is not concerned with the trivial details of Bible, but, rather, with the story of the living God with us, giving "meaning to the whole human enterprise."[46] Second, black preaching interprets the Bible within the hermeneutic of freedom. Black preaching, says he, understands the Bible as a present-tense liberating gospel, not a

---

42. Simmons and Thomas, *Sacred Fire*, 8.
43. Ibid.
44. Ibid., 8–9.
45. Buttrick, "A Fearful Pulpit," 42–43.
46. Ibid.

The Nature of Life-Situation Preaching

"once-upon-a-time" expression of God.[47] Thus the Bible is relevant for today's liberation campaign.

Grappling with the applicability of life-situation preaching for African-Americans, Buttrick maintains that Fosdick's life-situation preaching never took hold in the black preaching enterprise because Fosdick's "implicit individualism"—sermons aimed at the individual selves—was incongruent with the lives of African-Americans who share a common reality of blackness in a racist society. I will concede that African-American preaching never fully took hold of Fosdick's life-situation preaching, and for the reason Buttrick suggests. However, I think this has more to do with accessibility than applicability. Martin Luther King Jr. was able to access Fosdick's sermons in printed form and apply his techniques to sermons because he had access to college, university, and seminary libraries. During Fosdick's heyday, most African-Americans were not college educated. Many relied heavily on keen memorization skills to capture words and thoughts. I do not think that King is an exception to the rule in terms of his strategic use of Fosdick's preaching method, but, rather, a beneficiary and model of the effectiveness of life-situation preaching for African-American listeners.

I want to give equal voice to Leonora Tisdale, a white female homiletician, who describes Fosdick's life-situation preaching as prophetic preaching. In *Prophetic Preaching*, Tisdale defines prophetic preaching not as the type of preaching that predicts the future or deals with the end time, but as preaching that addresses public and social concerns.[48] She identifies Fosdick as a prophet because he had a pastoral heart. He modeled how to be prophetic while being hospitable. "The more deeply he came to know his flock," says Tisdale, "the more deeply he became aware of their suffering."[49] She notes further that Fosdick reminds us that "it is possible to advocate strongly for a cause without at the same time condemning those who disagree" with us, and that it "is possible to speak up boldly for peace without at the same time condemning those who are caught up in the complexities of war."[50] He displayed a concern for the personal and social dynamics of people's lives—a concern that he addressed through prophetic preaching. Fosdick understood and valued the individual in the community. His concern for and love for the individual makes him a "courageous prophetic

---

47. Ibid.
48. Tisdale, *Prophetic Preaching*, 3.
49. Ibid., 30.
50. Ibid., 31.

witness."[51] "Because Fosdick cared passionately about individuals," writes Tisdale, "he also cared about the systems that affect a person's life—be they theological (as in the fundamentalist/modernist debate) or political (as in his stance on pacifism)."[52] He performed exegesis of the human person by analyzing persons in their contexts so that he could apply the gospel in relevant ways to their unique personal and social contexts.

Tisdale argues that the church needs more "contextual preaching," which she defines as, "preaching which not only gives serious attention to the interpretation of biblical texts, but which gives equally serious attention to the interpretation of congregations and their sociocultural contexts; preaching which not only aims toward greater 'faithfulness' to the gospel of Jesus Christ, but which also aims toward greater 'fittingness' (in content, form and style) for a particular congregational gathering of hearers."[53] She advocates a balanced approach to preaching that takes congregational context as seriously as biblical exegesis and denominational doctrine. Her description of Fosdick's approach to preaching is helpful in that it explains the importance of addressing the systems that affect a person's life, and it is helpful in that it explicates the importance of analyzing persons in their contexts so that the gospel can be applied in relevant ways to their personal and social context. This description of Fosdick's preaching is beneficial to our discussion of life-situation preaching for African-Americans' unique social issues.

At any rate, however we define or describe preaching—personal identification with the existential situation of the listeners, a sermon that addresses public and social concerns, or exegesis of persons in their contexts, for example—it must take seriously the life situations of listeners. Although different ethnic groups face unique challenges in life, life-situation preaching effectively addresses their personal and social problems on their own terms in language with which they are familiar. The sociocultural context for African-Americans is quite different from, say, Jewish or Irish people, and vice versa. Much of African-American preaching is life-situation preaching, as it speaks to the social, economic, political, and physical well-being of America's black masses. As we will see, life-situation preaching and African-American preaching have many indistinguishable similarities. As preaching has lost its centrality in white mainline churches, black

---

51. Ibid., 37.
52. Ibid.
53. Tisdale, *Preaching as Local Theology and Folk Art*, 33.

The Nature of Life-Situation Preaching

preaching continues to survive and thrive in the twenty-first century. What do African-American teachers of preaching have to say about preaching to contemporary listeners' life situations? Following is an all too brief discussion on a number of well-known African-American homiliticians and their views on African-American preaching. These homiliticians and/or preachers speak to the importance of preaching that addresses listener's needs and life situations. They are discussed generationally.

Henry H. Mitchell

A hermeneutic principle articulated by Henry H. Mitchell, long considered the father of African-American homiletics, is the idea that the gospel must speak to people's current needs.[54] This principle in black preaching has historical significance. According to Mitchell, "the Black ancestors felt no compulsion to be orthodox or accepted. They showed no inclination to follow literalistic interpretations such as those devised to justify slavery. On the contrary, they looked without vested bias for answers to Black people's needs."[55] African-American preaching seeks to carve out a black hermeneutic that is unapologetically faithful to the unique thoughts and interpretations of the Bible that grow out of the black religious experience. It addresses the African-American experience in America and is strongly committed to changing it. For Mitchell, the sermon is not designed to be merely an intellectual product to enlighten listeners; rather, it is designed to bring life to and sustain life for African-Americans. "There is a radical difference," he says, "between listening to an essay designed to enlighten and listening to a Word desperately needed to sustain life."[56] African-American congregations benefit from preaching that is down-to-earth and not pseudosophisticated or pseudointellectual. Down-to-earth or practical preaching meets people where they are intellectually and educationally by being sensitive to the different educational levels and professional backgrounds represented in a congregation on any given Sunday.

---

54. Mitchell, *Black Preaching*, 20. Mitchell has contributed inestimably to the field of preaching. He has been the greatest champion of African-American preaching for over three decades.

55. Ibid., 21.

56. Ibid. Mitchell sounds remarkably like Fosdick on this point. Fosdick criticized his contemporaries' preaching because their sermons resembled an essay on a subject matter, with no real connection to or contact with human living.

Life-Situation Preaching for African-Americans

In proclaiming the gospel to African-Americans' life situations, black preaching is centered in the authority of the Bible. Noting the exception to the rule, Mitchell observed that occasionally a black congregation would entertain black preaching that is topical in nature. The best of black preaching, Mitchell holds, is based on biblical authority and biblical insights.[57] He qualifies this statement by noting that African-Americans are not oblivious to scientific insights regarding literalism in biblical interpretation such as "bibliolaters," "idolaters," or "inerrantists." Unlike the modernist-fundamentalist controversy that ensued in Fosdick's day, African-American preaching is not in the mode of either "modernists" or "fundamentalists," notes Mitchell.[58] For African-Americans, the word of God filled the void once occupied by an authoritative oral tradition.

In the African-American preaching tradition, the preacher is concerned with the existential problems of African-Americans. One of the indubitable points on which African-American homileticians agree is that African-American preaching must place primary emphasis on the immediate needs and existential experiences of African-Americans. Any preaching in the African-American religious context that does not take seriously such critical things is merely religious talk devoid of substance and relevance. "The Black preacher," says Mitchell, "has had to give strength for the current day's journey, the guidance and vision for extended survival in an absurdly trying existence."[59] The African-American congregation wants to know what the gospel says about their struggles and hardships. Regarding the congregation's sermonic expectations, Mitchell states: "The Black worshipper is seeking the answers to visceral questions on which life itself depends. The solution of abstract problems can wait. The important questions are more pragmatic and immediate."[60] There is a distinctive difference between sermons that are designed to help people live godly lives—spiritual formation, character development—and sermons that are designed to help people stay alive, human preservation and survival. The latter has a sense of urgency that is unmistakably palpable, although an effective sermon will incorporate both of these elements.

Mitchell notes that the introduction of an African-American sermon consists of an important issue with which listeners can identify immediately.

---

57. Ibid., 56.
58. Ibid., 57.
59. Ibid., 105.
60. Ibid., 127.

The Nature of Life-Situation Preaching

This observation speaks directly to the similarities between African-American peaching and life-situation preaching. Although the former may not start with the Bible, it is Bible-centered. Such a claim may cause some to question the former's fidelity to Scripture. This particular element of the African-American sermon in no way diminishes the importance or centrality of the Bible in African-American preaching. Similar to Fosdick's life-situation preaching for white people, African-American preaching gives primary emphasis to the immediate needs of black people.[61]

African-American preaching has distinguishable qualities. These qualities include *practicality* in its delivery and theological application; *applicability* to African-Americans' existential life situations; and *actionability* in terms of its consequences. That is, African-American preaching has practical value insofar as it necessitates action (social, political, humanitarian, philanthropic). In addition, it is practical in the sense that it is unencumbered by pretentious academic jargon. Mitchell acknowledges as much when he says that the African-American preacher must declare the gospel in the vernacular of the people and resist the temptation to sound learned and proper.[62] In a real sense, such a preacher faces a bicultural linguistic dilemma. Mitchell clarifies this point, saying: "They must be fluent in Black language [a system of communication that is unique to and true to African-Americans] for this is fundamental to their calling, and yet they must also be fluent in standard English, because they must communicate beyond their congregation. Their language must be black enough to generate rapport with the congregation by means of an identity which is perceived as close. They must be able to touch the souls of Black folk with soul language, putting them at ease and gaining greatest access by avoiding the linguistic signals of social distance."[63] Thus, the African-American preacher must be bicultural and bilingual to reach African-American listeners and to communicate with non-African-Americans inside and outside the congregation. The most notable preachers from the African-American homiletical tradition, including but not limited to Martin Luther King Jr., Gardner C. Taylor, Prathia L. Hall, James Alexander Forbes Jr., Cheryl Sanders, Teresa L. Fry Brown, Charles E. Booth, Carolyn Ann Knight,[64] to name a few, have

---

61. Ibid., 128.

62. Ibid., 20.

63. Ibid., 81. Some of the features of "Black English" include a slower rate of delivery, simpler sentence structure, and tonal inflections (84).

64. See LaRue, *Power*, for a list of notable African-American preachers. Such a list

been able to communicate effectively in diverse ethnic contexts because they have mastered the cultural distinctiveness, idiomatic phrases, vocabulary, and preaching tradition of African-American and white audiences.

The fact of the matter is that it is difficult to preach effectively to African-Americans without understanding their culture, language, vocabulary, communal life, and life situations. What is meant by "preach effectively" is that the preaching is understandable, relatable, and actionable to African-American listeners. The unique experience of African-Americans calls for a critical engagement with the complexity and reality of life as descendants of enslaved Africans. In the African-American religious community, the church has been at the center of life and existence, a truth that has been proclaimed at least since the time of W. E. B. DuBois, who said in 1900: "The Negro church of to-day is the social center of Negro life in the United States, and the most characteristic expression of African character."[65] From major civil and human rights campaigns to refuge from oppression and everyday life situations, the African-American church has been a bastion of culture and heritage, and a beacon of hope in difficult times. The African-American church may be viewed as monolithic, but it is a socially and economically diverse institution within the larger religious community. Be that at it may, the spirit of the African-American church is unmistakably united in solidarity for the betterment of life for the community to which it belongs.

Church attendance and membership differs according to urban or rural location and the social demographics of the members, especially as it relates to the number of college-educated professionals. Such congregants often times prefer a seminary-trained preacher, as they are accustomed to a particular discourse that may be absent in a non-seminarian-trained preacher. The same may be said of congregations with fewer college-educated members. These members appreciate a preacher who is able to communicate in culturally relevant terminology. These rules are not hard and fast, though. A congregation that consists of many college-educated professionals, for example, may call a non-seminary-trained preacher to serve as pastor. The main distinction between the two genres is formal education, but this does not settle the matter. Equally important, if not more

---

is inexhaustible, but certain names should not be omitted from any list of preaching extraordinaires: Sandy Ray, C. L. Franklin, Samuel D. Proctor, William Holmes Borders, Ella Mitchell, Howard Thurman, Benjamin E. Mays, J. Alfred Smith Sr., Charles G. Adams, Katie Cannon, Vashti Murphy McKenzie, and many others.

65. See DuBois, "The Religion of the American Negro," 216.

The Nature of Life-Situation Preaching

so, is the preacher's ability to communicate in the language and idioms of African-American culture.

Henry Mitchell has posited that seminary-trained clergy who are adept at both standard American English and Black English are more effective and in greater demand.[66] Rightfully so. Even more thought provoking, he noted that "whenever a substantial number of Black-culture churches have been faced with the choice between a preacher who can communicate with them or one who is seminary trained, they have chosen communication over education."[67] Mitchell's point is that the African-American preacher must be able to communicate in the vernacular of those to whom she preaches. He went as far as to say that no free black church will ever call a pastor who cannot speak the language of the congregation. It is doubtful that this assertion will stand the test of time. As the digital revolution changes the way in which we communicate, there will undoubtedly be a need for innovative communicators, well-versed in the language of the times as well as the language of the congregation. Formal training is critical to mastering the preaching apparatus and tools to effectively communicate the gospel, but this should not hinder the preacher from communicating to the audience in the language that they understand. Formal educational training in a white seminary does not guarantee that an African-American will get a pastorate, for churches have a proclivity toward calling a preacher who is a product of their own denominational engineering.

For African-American preachers, learning to preach is an activity that involves the church community. Many learn to preach primarily through emulation of accomplished preachers. Young preachers observe the hermeneutics and homiletics of mature preachers, who have mastered the art of preaching. While the white church places primary emphasis on educational training, the African-American church places emphasis on practical training in an ecclesiastical context. Cleophus J. LaRue, who will be discussed shortly, highlights the difference in methodology and pedagogy in preacher formation for African-American preachers. Said LaRue, "For the most part, whites in mainline and high-church congregations are declared fit to preach once they have successfully completed the degree requirements of a bona fide theological institution and passed the basic exams required by their particular judicatories."[68] He expounds: "In many white churches one

---

66. Mitchell, *Black Preaching*, 79.
67. Ibid., 80.
68. LaRue, *Testify*, 29.

is declared fit to preach through *certification*. In the black church one is declared fit to preach through *demonstration*."[69] In some African-American churches, the lack of formal education does not preclude a preacher from a preaching assignment. These examples notwithstanding, the preacher and the church benefit from a preacher who has received a formal education and is grounded in church history, theology, ethics, homiletics, church administration, biblical studies, and other preacher-formation courses. I will say, though, that more and more churches are seeking seminary-trained, experienced African-Americans for pastorates. A fact that is corroborated by pastor-vacancy advertisements on denominational websites.[70] Most importantly, African-American churches want a preacher who can "preach." In the worship context, the sermon is the culmination of the praying, singing, praising, and worshipping. It is, to be sure, the apex of the liturgical experience, the celebration of hope in seemingly hopeless times. Although all elements of the worship service are important for the life and spirit of the church, everything is but preliminary to the sermon and nothing is more important.

James E. Massey

In *Designing the Sermon*, James Earl Massey (1930–2018) says that real preaching is rooted in God's concern for persons.[71] He describes such preaching as communication that is concerned with helping listeners to experience grace and the divine help that deals with "human sin and crippling experiences."[72] Real preaching, in Massey's view, is more than the proclamation of biblical statements; it is, to be sure, a "probe into the prevailing assumptions and beliefs which have determined the major problems of our time."[73] This means that the preacher must be cognizant of the problems

---

69. Ibid., 30.

70. A case in point is the pastor-vacancy announcements on the National Baptist Convention, USA, Inc. website. As of June 20, 2019, the website featured eighty-one senior pastor vacancies. Of the eighty-one vacancies, 38% (31) did not specify the minimum educational requirement; 4% (3) required an associate degree; 28% (23) required a bachelor's degree or its equivalency; and 30% (24) required formal theological education, a master's degree or its equivalency. On average, churches sought candidates with at least five years of pastoral experience. Other denominational websites yield similar findings.

71. Massey, *Sermon*, 15.

72. Ibid., 16.

73. Ibid., 17.

The Nature of Life-Situation Preaching

and thoughts of those to whom she preaches. Real preaching challenges the status quo rather than upholding it. Massey explains it this way: "So we design our sermons and preach them—not to preserve a world or protect it, but to create a new order through announcing hope for change and bidding all to accept and act upon that hope and need."[74] In Massey's line of thought, real preaching is vital; that is, it deals with real people's needs and offers help from a real God. In terms of sermon design, Massey is less rigid than most homileticians and preachers. For him, a sermon can be preached to offer a solution to a problem, to teach doctrine, to address spiritual or social ills, to support a cause, or to sustain listeners.[75]

Massey notes that the central goal in preaching is to relate the gospel to the listener's life. "Any sermon," writes Massey, "will have increased appeal when an increased understanding of the listener and his or her personal world informs the planning behind it."[76] One of Massey's guiding homiletical principles for shaping a sermon is to begin with a human issue or divine claim—"some human condition to which one must speak or some divine concern to which one must point the hearer's attention."[77] Unlike Fosdick who maintained that every sermon should have for its main business the solving of some vital problem, Massey advocated an either-or approach to sermon design. The takeaway here is not so much the importance of the design or structure of the sermon as it is the purpose and goal of the sermon. Regardless of whether the preacher starts with a human issue or divine claim, the primary goal is to relate the gospel to the listener's life.

As is the case in Fosdick's life-situation preaching, Massey explains that ideas for sermons can come from something read, from some visit, from a congregational need, or from counseling experiences.[78] Such activities and experiences for Massey provide insight into human concerns and needs, as it did for Fosdick, in that his counseling experiences enriched his preaching ministry. His ministry, as discussed, was the product of life-situation preaching and pastoral counseling. Both Massey and Fosdick agree that pastoral counseling is the supreme activity to gain insight into human nature and personality. Perhaps it is true, as Barbara Brown Taylor has said, that if the preacher is also the congregation's priest and pastor, then the

---

74. Ibid., 17.
75. Ibid., 17.
76. Ibid., 25.
77. Ibid., 30.
78. Ibid., 30.

"quality of their life together—the memories, conversations, experiences, and hopes they share—is the fabric from which the sermon is made."[79]

Gardner C. Taylor

While a student at Shaw Divinity School in 2007, I had the privilege to learn from the Reverend Gardner Calvin Taylor (1918–2015). I took his course on preaching. I can still hear his baritone voice urging students to "aim, aim, aim!" Although he has never been identified as a life-situation preacher, the similarities in homiletical theory between his and Fosdick's are unmistakably clear. Some of his most crucial remarks regarding preaching are contained in the fifth volume of his six-volume series, compiled and edited by Edward L. Taylor. The fifth volume features Taylor's lectures, essays, and interviews. Herein we find Taylor's definitive words on sermon composition and delivery. After forty years of preaching, Taylor still believed that "a sermon usually has a better chance in our biblically illiterate time if it begins with a 'cool introduction' in which the secret, or purpose, of the sermon is suggested but not exposed."[80] He also believed that the introduction to a sermon "ought to touch the hearers at a point of concern or interest in their lives."[81] In Taylor's homiletics, the issues that concern the structuring of a sermon includes the preacher's own faith about Scripture, the preacher's personality, and the intent and type of passage chosen for the text, each of which is briefly discussed below.

With respect to the preacher's faith about Scripture, one's theological belief about Scripture affects one's understanding and interpretation of the Bible. Therefore, according to Taylor, the preacher has to strike the right balance between fundamentalism and liberalism. The fundamentalist stance relies too much on the authority of Scripture and tradition while the liberalist stance relies too much on human thought. Taylor exposes the weaknesses of each approach. On the one hand, "If one sees Scripture as being word for word, accent by accent, incident by incident, genealogy by genealogy, the precise word of God, then the sermon is likely to take on a quality of *ex cathedra* pronouncement."[82] The point is, a sermon can be so textually focused that it fails to establish a vital connection with its

---

79. Taylor, *Preaching Life*, 82.
80. Taylor, "Shaping Sermons," 48.
81. Ibid.
82. Ibid., 43.

The Nature of Life-Situation Preaching

listeners' lives. On the other hand, "If the preacher believes that sermons are only the most elevated human literature, then the sermon is likely to ignore the mysteries of God's self-disclosures which are the very kernel of biblical material."[83] Exploring both sermon options, Taylor maintains that a sermon has the greatest chance of accomplishing its purpose when it arises out of the preacher's own faith.

Regarding the preacher's personality, Taylor notes that it affects the interpretation and delivery of a sermon. Fact is, some texts are simply better suited for some people than for others. The beauty of the preaching enterprise is that various preachers with distinct personalities can each preach the same text with ingenuity of interpretation and presentation. "It is the glory of preaching that one text can be given as many different nuances, all of them loyal to the Scriptures, as there are preachers dealing with them,"[84] notes Taylor. The sermon is as much a reflection of the preacher's personality as the preacher's personality is a reflection of the sermon. The two are inextricably linked. Taylor notes that Fosdick's pulpit work reflects a "deep piety and great loyalty" that never would have been possible if he did not suffer a nervous breakdown for which he was institutionalized for three months in an Elmira sanitarium. This experience and the sensitivity that caused it had much to do with the great preaching gift of Fosdick and his capacity to reach people at their depths, observes Taylor.[85] The preaching event is in essence a matter of the preacher communicating the truth and relevance of the Bible for the life situations of the diverse personalities occupying the pews. Therefore, Taylor cautions that "the preacher needs to consider himself or herself in relation to the text, whatever it may be, in order to guard against attempting, on the one hand, what is unnatural, and on the other hand, what is merely eccentric."[86]

As regards the intent and type of passage chosen for the text, Taylor says that a sermon must stay true to the intent and meaning of the passage in its original setting. A discussion of Taylor's hermeneutics is beyond the scope of this book. Suffice it to say, Taylor believed that the conscientious preacher will avoid misinterpreting and misapplying a text. Dealing with the text contextually does not mean that the preacher cannot exercise imaginative intelligence in interpreting and preaching the text. It does mean,

83. Ibid.
84. Ibid., 44.
85. See Taylor, "Building the Sermon," 181; see also Taylor, "Black Patriarchs," 217.
86. See Taylor, "Shaping Sermons," 45.

however, that the preacher's sermon ought to be authorized by and faithful to the biblical text. It is bad when a sermon lacks scriptural underpinnings and even worse when it takes a text out of context and uses it wrongly.

Taylor hints at the application of *eisegesis* in interpreting and misusing the text. Eisegesis is the process of interpreting a text by "reading into" the text in such a way that it exposes one's predispositions and presuppositions. Essentially, the interpreter imposes his or her own meaning onto and into the text, despite the context and original intent of the author. What Taylor advises, simply put, is sound exegesis—a critical explanation or interpretation of a text based on its social-historical context and authorial intent, observing the setting and surroundings thereof. Taylor cites an anonymous preacher who phrases the exegetical process creatively, all the while asking thought-provoking, sermon-enhancing questions:

> A wise preacher of another generation suggested that one ought to "walk up and down the street on which a text lives." The surrounding terrain ought to be taken into account. What is the block like on which the text is located? Is it a rundown section, or does it sparkle with a neat tidiness? Is the sky overhead leaden or gray, or is it bright and sunlit? Does one hear light and merry music in the neighborhood of the text, or are there solemn cadences of some sad and mournful time? One need not get lost in the atmosphere, but a sense of climate will greatly aid the sermon in breathing with life and having, therefore, an interest for living people.[87]

I need not explicate the obvious. I should note, though, that Taylor is encouraging preachers to be faithful to exegesis, as it yields certain benefits. First, the movement of the text itself can determine the structure of the sermon. Second, and even more suggestive, the movement of the text can provide an outline and structure for those who would like to preach without a manuscript. In Taylor's theory of preaching, "the structure, design, and delivery of the sermon ought to breathe with the awareness that it is doing business in the supreme matters of human life."[88] He explains further, "It ought not be trivial or fancy or syrupy or mean or truckling to any human pride or pretense."[89] For Taylor, the task and purpose of the sermon ought to be intelligible. The task is to bring the gospel to bear on the issues and

---

87. Ibid., 46.
88. Ibid., 48.
89. Ibid.

The Nature of Life-Situation Preaching

concerns of human life while the purpose is to reach the hearts and minds of listeners, bringing them before the transformative presence of God.

Therefore, it is the preacher's duty to bring the word of God to the people of God and to have them intersect. Describing the preacher's obligation, Taylor says, "Our responsibility is to bring that which is given to that which is happening and to have them intersect."[90] For African-Americans, this means bringing the gospel into dialogue with the profound problems and social conditions of black existence that affect their lives, livelihood, neighborhoods, and communities. In Taylor's view, the greatness of America notwithstanding, America is still a disunited nation split along the lines of race, class, gender, sexual orientation, age, etc. "This country, with all of the incalculable resources, the immeasurable riches, natural and human, and with a political creed among the most hallowed with which the mind of man has ever dealt and the societies of man have ever wrestled, blessed in countless ways, still is a nation torn and divided,"[91] notes Taylor. What makes for decisive preaching in the face of such conditions is "a willingness to forsake skimming the surface and to look into the abyss of our human situation, to deal with the splendor and the squalor of our humanity, the grandeur and the grime, always with a glance up at him who connects these two."[92] A case in point is racism, as Taylor explains: "Racism is set against the one-blood tie which God ordained in our creation. Racism, whether it is the rapacity of a majority position or the reactionary toughness and terrorism of an outraged minority, assaults the mandate of our creation that we human beings are to have dominion over . . . every living creature that crawls on the earth, not over each other."[93]

Preaching at its best confronts the destructive sins of our society while challenging the community's delinquencies and derelictions. Taylor, like Fosdick, was concerned to show the relevance of the gospel for a particular listener who was struggling with specific issues. The point of homiletical intersection for both preachers is the belief that at the heart of preaching is the preacher's ability to establish a vital connection with listeners by understanding and addressing their issues, interests, and concerns through the medium of preaching. Taylor and Fosdick share many affinities and

90. Taylor, "Contemporary Preaching," 96.
91. Taylor, "Preaching in the Urban Situation," 94.
92. Taylor, "Preaching Responsibility," 102.
93. Taylor, "Preaching the Whole Counsel of God," 189. This is a paraphrase of Genesis 2:26.

similarities as it relates to their respective homiletical theories. Both preachers have inspired many an earnest preacher to excellence in preaching. A superb study, which is beyond the purpose here, would be a comparison of both preachers' homiletics.

Katie G. Cannon

In *Teaching Preaching*, Katie Geneva Cannon (1950–2018), the late Annie Scales Rogers Professor of Christian Ethics at Union Presbyterian Seminary, presents the distinct homiletical method of Isaac Rufus Clark Sr. Clark taught homiletics at the Interdominational Theological Center, Atlanta, Georgia. In her articulation of Clark's method, Cannon presents a critique of contemporary preaching that resembles Fosdick's in content and substance. An honest critique of the preaching situation, she argues, is important for one's preaching ministry. This is especially true of black preaching. "And we especially want to make an honest critique of the black preaching situation, since we are definitely interested in the meaning and implications of preaching for future black liberation," she writes.[94] It is instructive to note that Cannon's presentation of Clark's critique entails an assessment of black preaching's meaning and implications for black liberation. Black preaching at its best is concerned with the liberation of African-Americans from the chains and shackles of racism and white supremacy.

Black preaching speaks to the existential realities of the black experience in America. In clear terms, Cannon writes: "We definitely want to see what and how and why preaching can help black folks to really overcome in this land of ours through our preaching."[95] Black preaching at its best helps African-Americans to live victoriously in a land where they face the constant threat of defeat and even death. Such preaching gets at the central nervous system of black life and black existence in America. To say that black preaching gets at the central nervous system is to say that it is interested in matters that are central to African-Americans, whose weary backs bear the oppressive weight and hardships of black existence in white America.

Clark's critique of the then-contemporary preaching situation is relevant to today's preaching. Influenced by Albert Knudson's critique of the theology of his day, Cannon says that preaching is "shallow and in

---

94. Cannon, *Teaching Preaching*, 54. Cannon was the first African-American woman ordained in the United Presbyterian Church (U.S.A.).

95. Ibid.

The Nature of Life-Situation Preaching

the shadows."[96] Using these terms, "shallow and in the shadows," Cannon assesses the contemporary preaching situation. In her assessment of contemporary preaching as "shallow," she says that much of contemporary preaching does not get at the deep, fundamental, serious questions of life that most people are concerned about. It lacks content and substance as it relates to life situations. Cannon's critique is helpful:

> Much contemporary preaching is often lacking divine depth and human depth. No sound theology is in it and no understanding of sound psychology or sociology is under it. There is often no great import, divine or human, in much of today's crap-trap. There is often no profound impact on the thinking and behavior of people in their living today. In that sense, much of today's preaching is about as deep as a single dewdrop on the desert sand at high noon, shallow. Pish! There is a drop of dew out there, but you don't even know that it is out there.[97]

Cannon's comprehensive assessment of the contemporary preaching situation starts with the preacher's lack of commitment to the task of preaching. First, she notes, the preacher fails to avail oneself of the tools of theology, sociology, and psychology, intelligently bringing these disciplines to bear on life situations. Second, she observes, the preaching does not encourage or motivate people to change their thinking or behavior. Preaching that touches the emotions only can be overly sentimental; and preaching that touches the intellect only can be overly academic. Black preaching that is undergirded with intelligent thought, diligent study, and fervent prayer can provide divine depth and human depth to contemporary preaching. Such preaching is in tune with and sensitive to the life situations of African-Americans.

In her assessment of contemporary preaching as "in the shadows," she says that many preachers do take their preaching responsibility seriously. Consequently, much contemporary preaching does not shed light on deep issues and questions of life. Preaching, which was once the highlight of the Protestant worship experience, has been peripheralized for music and drama. Cannon counsels that the unprepared preacher has no business in the pulpit. Her hortative counsel need not fall on deaf ears: "Don't let no devil fool you out of your place in the pulpit. There is only one time when the devil ought to fool you out of the pulpit, and that is when you ain't got no

---

96. Ibid., 55.
97. Ibid.

Life-Situation Preaching for African-Americans

message. Sit down and let the choir take over, for maybe they can sing some gospel."[98] Cannon's is a stringent critique, acerbic even, but a necessary one. Preachers who do not take seriously the responsibility to study and devote time to prayer and meditation should reassess their choice of vocation.

The correlation between disciplined preparation and a quality sermon is not lost on Cannon: "You can tell that by the time preachers give to preparing to preach. Some fools think that they can get a sermon together in two or three hours. They are crazy. It will take the average one of you, if you really do it right, it will take you about forty to sixty hours."[99] Admittedly, this is intimidating for any preacher, especially a young or novice preacher. The amount of time for sermon preparation will invariably differ from one preacher to another. Undoubtedly, though, preaching at its best takes hard work, disciplined study, and time.

Thought provokingly, Cannon likens sermon preparation to Jacob's encounter with a mysterious divine being at Peniel in the book of Genesis (32:22–32). In this narrative, Jacob epitomizes the people of Israel, who strive with God and humans perennially. Jacob wrestles with the divine being. Unable to prevail against Jacob, the divine being dislocated Jacob's hip. This did not deter Jacob. He fought all the more valiantly. Finally, the divine being demanded that Jacob let him go, as morning was upon them, but Jacob refused to let go without receiving a blessing. The committed preacher is willing to wrestle with the text and ponder a sermon until the preacher is blessed from the encounter. Simply put, the composition of a sermon is hard yet rewarding work. The reward is that it will bless the preacher and change listeners' thinking and behavior.

What Cannon makes clear is that African-American preaching, similar to life-situation preaching, must address the particularities of the African-American experience. To this end, African-American preachers must be committed to preaching that is aware of and speaks to the existential depths, complexities, and realities of the black existence in America, for this is the heart and uniqueness of black preaching. "You got to know what you got to do if you are about liberation," advises Cannon.[100] Hence, black preaching must get close enough to human experience to effect liberation.

---

98. Ibid., 56.
99. Ibid., 54.
100. Ibid.

The Nature of Life-Situation Preaching
Frank A. Thomas

Highlighting the dichotomy between educated and uneducated preachers in the African-American preaching tradition, Frank A. Thomas, the Nettie Sweeney and Hugh Th. Miller Professor of Homiletics at Christian Theological Seminary, points to the two competing genres of "folk preaching" and "intellectual preaching."[101] The former consists of old-time preaching, while the latter consists of "educated preaching." Thomas keenly notes that the best African-American preachers are able to combine both genres in their preaching. Many of the earliest African-American preachers had to imitate the models and tradition of Euro-American preachers. Indeed, a critique of my book is that it uses a Euro-American preaching model—the life-situation preaching model of Fosdick—to address the African-American preaching tradition. This critique is not without merit.

The preaching in white churches, as is true of organized religion, is filtered through Euro-American norms and customs. Enslaved Africans were forced to accept the religion of their white enslavers. Religion was used as a means to compel obedience and submissiveness. Thomas observes as much in his study on African-American preaching: "Every preaching tradition, including African-American preaching, has models that because of their excellence in manifesting the tradition are considered to be worthy of imitation. In the African-American preaching tradition, performers of the tradition observe and learn directly from these models more than the application of rules or homiletical textbooks."[102] What Thomas makes clear is that there are preaching traditions and models that are indeed worthy of imitation. I would argue further that any preaching tradition or model that speaks intelligently to the life situations of African-Americans is worthy of practical consideration. This speaks to the indispensability of life-situation preaching. The historical and contemporary relevance of Fosdick's preaching ministry is not lost on Thomas.

This is seen most clearly in Thomas's discussion on Martin Luther King Jr. Thomas observes that King "merged parts of liberal white (Fosdick, Hamilton, Bosely) and African-American intellectual and educated preaching traditions (Johnson, Mays, Johns) with African-American (many unnamed and illiterate) folk preaching traditions to create a discourse that spoke to most Americans and contributed to significant social change in

---

101. Thomas, *African-American Preaching*, 11.
102. Ibid., 17.

Life-Situation Preaching for African-Americans

America."[103] The beauty and potency of King's preaching stemmed from his creativity in merging the best in Euro-American and African-American preaching traditions. What was the result of this creative merging of traditions? In merging the two traditions, he was able to overcome the limitations inherent in each tradition and forge a more excellent homiletic. Fosdick's influence on King's thinking about and approach to preaching should not be overlooked. In fact, Thomas names Fosdick as one of the twentieth-century preachers who "raised serious questions and forced rethinking about the dominant rational homiletical paradigm."[104] As a young preacher, King was unquestionably influenced by Fosdick. When it came time for the eighteen-year-old King to preach his trial sermon at Ebenezer, he burrowed his first sermon from Harry Emerson Fosdick's "Life is What you Make It."[105] Fosdick's published sermons would serve King well throughout his life. It is known, for example, that King owned no less than six of Fosdick's collections of sermons in his personal library.[106] Without a doubt, King used speeches, excerpts, phrases, and illustrations from Fosdick's sermons, usually without attribution.

To be sure, Keith D. Miller argues that King "borrowed materials" and even plagiarized Fosdick, not to mention other notable white and black preachers such as Phillips Brooks, George Buttrick, Howard Thurman, and Wallace Hamilton.[107] Miller has documented the sources of King's writings. In a personal interview with King, Mervyn A. Warren questioned King about his sermon structure. King conveyed to Warren that Fosdick influenced the three-part arrangement of his sermons.[108] At any rate, suffice it to say that King's use of Fosdick's sermonic materials and structure speaks emphatically to the importance of life-situation preaching—it's structure, content, practical approach to preaching, and emphasis on human needs—for the preacher and for African-American listeners. That King borrowed from other preachers (as well as scholars in his case) is not surprising given that many preachers, regardless of ethnicity, tend to borrow from colleagues without acknowledging the source of their work. Richard Lischer comes to King's defense, writing that Miller's analysis exaggerates the extent to which

---

103. Ibid., 30.
104. Ibid., 61.
105. Lischer, *King*, 28.
106. See Carson, et al. eds., *Papers*, 6:636–37.
107. Miller, *Voice of Deliverance*, 229.
108. Warren, *King Came Preaching*, 154.

The Nature of Life-Situation Preaching

King relied on the words of other preachers, giving the impression that King was "neither original nor ethical in his use of secondary sources."[109] On the contrary, argues Lischer, King used his peers' sermons for an idea, phrase, or outline.

Notwithstanding these issues, King was able to apply the best elements of life-situation preaching to the black religious experience to meet the immediate felt needs of African-Americans and others who enjoyed his peaching. The black preaching tradition is too multifaceted and multifarious to be defined in definitive language. LaRue notes, for example, the definitional challenges with black preaching, as it were: "With respect to the question of what constitutes 'black preaching,' there is a very powerful and settled school of thought among black preachers that says there is no such thing as black preaching per se, with its own specific characteristics and distinctive traits. Those who maintain this view say there are black preachers who preach, but they don't preach black, they simply preach."[110]

In his research, Frank Thomas surveyed twenty-two homileticians who teach and publish scholarship on African-American preaching, and twenty-five African-Americans pastors, who preach on a regular basis. A question of interest was, "What is black preaching?" The response to this question is quite telling. The survey participants concluded that the question might never be settled definitively. The African-American preaching tradition, they acknowledged, "has been shaped by faithful responses to centuries of racial, sexual, social, cultural, political, economic, and gender oppression, and as a result, is uniquely able to minister to all people, and especially hurting and oppressed people, in America and all over the globe."[111] We may conclude, then, that black preaching consists of more than one's ethnicity, more than one manner of pulpit presentation, more than homileticians' sense of what good preaching is, and more than one definition. There are, however, distinctive characteristics or features of this tradition that distinguishes it from other forms of preaching.

Cleophus J. LaRue

Noting the present-day plight of preaching in mainline churches, Cleophus J. LaRue, the Francis Landey Patton Professor of Homiletics at Princeton

---

109. Lischer, *King*, 109.

110. LaRue, "Two Ships Passing in the Night," 138.

111. Thomas, *African-American Preaching*, 129.

Life-Situation Preaching for African-Americans

Theological Seminary, maintains that black preaching "sprinted across the threshold into the twenty-first century in far better shape than much preaching in predominantly white churches."[112] He contends that the distinctive power of black preaching is a matter of "extraordinary experiences that have, among other results, forged a unique way of understanding the Bible and applying those insights in very practical ways."[113] African-Americans' historical and contemporary experiences in America are unique, and, as a result, they interpret Scripture differently from traditional understandings of Christianity among whites. I agree with LaRue on this point. However, while it is true that the centrality of the Bible is unmistakable in black preaching, it is also true that the existential life situations of African-American listeners is critically important. I hold that any preaching, especially black preaching, that fails to take seriously the lived experiences and existential context of its listeners is missing the homiletical mark. To this point, LaRue agues that African-Americans' sociocultural experiences have a profound effect on their interpretation and understanding of who God is and how God works.

Without question, then, the point of departure for black preaching is the historical and contemporary experiences of African-Americans, who continue to be subjected to a biased judicial system, debilitated schools, inadequate or no health care, low-paying jobs, inferior housing, racial discrimination, police brutality, inequality in education and employment, and social, economic, and political oppression. These experiences provide an interpretive lens through which African-Americans view Scripture and life. "It is," writes LaRue, "that vital interpretive encounter between scripture and the struggles of the marginalized that the search for distinctiveness in black preaching should begin."[114] In black preaching, the preacher, according to LaRue, believes that God is involved in the everyday affairs and circumstances of the marginalized, and that "God acts in very concrete and practical ways in matters pertaining to their survival, deliverance, advancement, prosperity, and overall well-being."[115]

LaRue further maintains that black preaching must emphasize what "blacks believe about God, scripture, and the *life situations* of those who

---

112. LaRue, "Two Ships," 127.
113. LaRue, *Black Preaching*, 1.
114. Ibid., 2.
115. Ibid., 3.

The Nature of Life-Situation Preaching

hear black preaching on a consistent basis" (author's italics).[116] The motif of a sovereign God who takes up the cause of the marginalized is salient in black preaching. LaRue asserts: "The God of the black church is conceived by the black religious tradition as being a responsive personal being with unquestioned, and unlimited, absolute power. Marginalized blacks have historically believed that a God who does not care does not count. Thus, a mighty God who takes up the cause of disposed African-Americans is the major premise that undergirds powerful black preaching."[117] African-Americans' interpretation of Scripture and understanding of God is derived from their unique sociocultural context.

According to LaRue, black preaching takes seriously God's concern for and involvement in the everyday affairs of African-Americans. Black preaching, as an art form, he writes, has been a potent force of social change, political empowerment, and spiritual renewal and transformation for the African-American community. To fully understand and appreciate black preaching, the reader must understand that African-Americans' interpretation and understanding of Scripture is colored by and interpreted through their unique historical and contemporary experiences of oppression, discrimination, and marginalization in America.[118] Advancing the point even further, LaRue writes: "As a direct result of their struggle against oppression, blacks have historically derived from scripture a central truth that there is a God of infinite power who can be trusted to act mightily on their behalf. This understanding comes out of almost four centuries of oppression and struggle."[119] Consequently, African-Americans' "life situations determine what blacks find redemptive in the scriptures, as opposed to some genre-specific [e.g., biblical narrative] partiality."[120] In the final analysis, the black homiletic tradition seeks to interpret and explain Scripture on behalf of marginalized and powerless African-Americans, and, in light of their social, economic, and political struggles, apply the gospel. This, I argue, is the intent of the life-situation sermon.

---

116. Ibid., 5.

117. Ibid.

118. In *Black Preaching*, Henry H. Mitchell calls African-Americans' approach to Scripture the "Black hermeneutic," which is the "unique thoughts and interpretations of the Bible that grow out of the Black religious experience..." (17).

119. LaRue, *Black Preaching*, 14–15.

120. Ibid., 15.

Life-Situation Preaching for African-Americans
Teresa L. Fry Brown

In *Weary Throats and New Songs*, Teresa L. Fry Brown, the Bandy Professor of Preaching at Candler School of Theology at Emory University, describes preaching as a dialogical process between God, the preacher, and the people of faith. This dialogical process is the essence of preaching. In her experience, it occurs in this manner: "The call of God through the preacher to the people of faith and the response channeled back to God through the preacher is the essence of the preaching."[121] In light of this dialogical process, the African-American preacher's role is to confront and change the status quo, the existential realities of black life. She instructs: "The role of the black preacher is to assist the listeners in the identification of spiritual, social, cultural, psychological, and economic issues that affect daily life. The sense of disenfranchisement stagnates personal pursuit of relationships, goals, and objectives. The preacher presents the realities of black life through a hermeneutic of suspicion, or examination of the status quo."[122] Fry Brown teaches her students to place themselves in the position of the congregation and to be aware of the lives of listeners. Not only must black preachers be aware of the lives of listeners, they must also be bold enough to address social issues that affect their lives. Candidly, she lectures: "The challenge of addressing social issues is absent in many contemporary black pulpits. I believe that part of the problem is the transitory nature of congregants, the distance between the preacher and the people, fear of confrontation, separation of the secular and the sacred, and belief that there is no need to address injustice, just the spiritual."[123] Her analysis is insightful.

For Fry Brown, the black preacher is not obligated to always address an issue or problem, but the preacher is obligated to "understand evil in all of its forms and power."[124] A sermon that misses the mark, that fails to address individual success, tragic events that affect everyone, or listeners' daily lives is, she asserts, irrelevant. She reminds us that the content of black preaching, historically speaking, has involved critiques of individuals, church, and society. In her homiletics theory, knowledge of the

---

121. Fry Brown, *Weary Throats and New Songs*, 9. In 2010, Fry Brown became the first African-American woman to attain the rank of full professor at Candler.

122. Ibid., 122.

123. Ibid., 123.

124. Ibid. Fry Brown discusses issues such as ageism, sexism, racism, and different success levels within the congregation as a part of her discussion on evil in all its forms and powers.

congregation is enhanced when preachers listen to congregants and understand their life situations. She points out as much, arguing that: "The preacher should be well-read in areas that affect the congregation. The preacher should empathetically reference the concerns of the congregation with care, yet challenge the congregation to look past the present circumstance to a God-ordained end."[125] Thus black preachers must have insight into human nature and the personal and social issues of listeners; and they must also be able to listen to, understand, and relate to people through lived experiences and empathetical pastoral care, while challenging listeners and the status quo.

In *Delivering the Sermon*, Fry Brown says that "preaching must involve an intimate, personal identification with the existential situation of the listeners, even to the point of gut-level emoting."[126] In her treatment of preaching, Fry Brown does not mention where she believes the sermon should start. She does, however, note that preaching "is communication in the concrete, filled with language and images from day-to-day details—dynamics, sights, sounds, smells, tastes, texture, and life scenes."[127] In such communication, it is important that the preacher recognizes and identifies with the listener's environment. There are two elements of Fry Brown's theory of preaching that are important to our unfolding understanding of life-situation preaching.

First, Fry Brown notes that preaching involves personal identification with the existential situation of the listeners which plays an important role in preaching. Second, preaching addresses day-to-day details of life, as previously discussed. Her description and analysis of preaching fits squarely with life-situation preaching, although she does not define preaching as such, but neither does Fosdick. For Fry Brown, the efficacy of the sermon lies in its ability to reinforce, correct, or transform "the convictions the listeners have as the speaker and the listener are invited to think again about beliefs."[128] In the final analysis, for Fry Brown a sermon should speak to existential life situations and transform the convictions of listeners. Any sermon that fails in this regard is irrelevant.

125. Ibid., 124.
126. Ibid., 8.
127. Ibid.
128. Ibid.

Life-Situation Preaching for African-Americans
Lisa L. Thompson

The life situations of black women provide a starting point for sermon development and preaching. Their stories and lived experiences inform preaching, enliven Christian worship, and strengthen communal belief and identity. In *Ingenuity: Preaching as an Outsider*, Lisa L. Thompson, the Cornelius Vanderbilt Chancellor Faculty Fellow of Black Homiletics and Liturgics at Vanderbilt Divinity School, points out that the experiences of black women, who she describes as the most vulnerable of our communities, require us to rethink practices of biblical interpretation and preaching. She extends an invitation to the faith community to imagine preaching through the lived experiences and realities of black women. Such individual and collective experiences provide a point of entry for the task of preaching, providing a catalyst for communal formation and transformation. Attending to the particularities of black women's lives, Thompson reminds her reader that, historically and existentially, people do not readily believe the voice and witness of black women preachers who are considered "forced outsiders," that is, pushed to the periphery of the African-American preaching tradition and pulpit, not to mention church, society, and other institutions and spaces.

For Thompson, giving voice to black women's particularities through preaching results in a distinctive communal formation sensitive to and informed by often unacknowledged and unconsulted realities of black women. She posits that the everyday realities of black women are primary resources for sermon development. Although often undervalued, if not ignored altogether, black women's life situations—concretized in the subtlety, complexity, and variety of their individual and collective experiences—provide intellectual and spiritual nourishment for the faith community. Indeed, Thompson argues that preaching that begins with the unique and varied experiences of black women takes seriously their lives and ministries, for preaching informs life as much as life informs preaching, and black women's lives are no exception.

Preaching to black women's life situations requires familiarity with the particularities of their unique experiences. To take seriously the lives of black women is to acknowledge that their experiences are "connected to a history that differentiates their experiences of racism from those of black men and their experiences of sexism from those of other women."[129]

---

129. Thompson, *Ingenuity*, 13.

The Nature of Life-Situation Preaching

Listening to and learning from black women's voices, experiences, and realities are fundamental to incorporating and transmuting the various raw materials of their lives into life-transforming preaching content. Thompson perspicaciously notes that listeners of sermons intuit what is valid by juxtaposing content with lived experiences. She notes further that listeners' lives, experiences, and acquired knowledge are the barometers used to judge the legitimacy of a sermon. For Thompson, then, the "lives of black women are a starting point for faithfully attending to the robustness of life and faith in a community."[130] As such, the preacher should consider the experiences and life situations of black women as important, relevant, and necessary for preaching.

Not only that, but the preacher should also deem black women's lived experiences as befittingly apropos for the task of preaching, especially as an entry point to sermon composition. To this point, Thompson instructively writes: "As the preacher begins with experience from the outset, they [sic] begin discerning right-fitting and meaningful possibilities of valid interpretations of scripture that honor the porous boundaries in the distinction between an ancient world and the world in which they lives [sic]."[131] In a very real sense, then, black women's lived experiences and life situations provide an ideal starting point for the task or preaching. Simply put, a preacher is doing serious business in the pulpit when the preacher is able to speak to the universality of life situations through the particular lens of black women's experiences.

The next chapter explores the theoretical foundation of Fosdick's sermon composition practice, provides insights into his life-situation preaching, and discusses his understanding of the purpose of a sermon.

130. Ibid., 38.
131. Ibid., 86.

3

Fosdick's Preaching Ministry

Fosdick's Preaching Theory and Practice

In *Building A Sermon*, Gardner Taylor observed that preaching in many so-called mainline churches is too flat, too horizontal, too colorless, and too unimaginative.[1] Taylor's poignant critique of preaching rings true today. All too often what is heard from the pulpit is recapitulations of topics or issues that have been thoroughly exhausted or recycled—the rehashing of practical matters in an unimaginative way. John Killinger also recognized this problem when he wrote that, "instead of appearing in the pulpit with cut-and-dried homilies, we need to come before people in common humanity and work with them toward the conclusions."[2] He stated further that, once done, "the conclusions will be personal and inescapable to them."[3] One can conclude from both preachers' comments that preaching should be imaginative, personal, and relevant to the lives of listeners. This is exactly what Fosdick sought to do. Given his success as a preacher, his theory and practice of preaching is worth our consideration.

Fosdick's words on his theory and practice of preaching have not been as plentiful as some would like. Although a prolific writer, he did not write a book-length account of his theory of preaching as such, much to

1. Taylor, "Building A Sermon," 172.
2. Killinger, *Preaching*, 35.
3. Ibid.

Fosdick's Preaching Ministry

the dismay of professional homileticians and clergy alike. This is unfortunate. However, we have enough sources to get a sense of the theoretical foundation of his sermon preparation and preaching practices. A synthesis of published articles and autobiographical remarks help to provide insight into his theory of preaching. Particularly helpful is Fosdick's chapter in his autobiography entitled "Learning How to Preach." Helpful also are articles such as "What Is the Matter With Preaching?"; "How I Prepare My Sermons"; and "Personal Counseling and Preaching." Taken together these sources distill the essence of his theory and practice of preaching. Each of these sources are consulted in order to develop a coherent picture of his approach to preaching.

Although often unconsulted and overlooked, Fosdick's inaugural address, "A Modern Preacher's Problem in His Use of the Scriptures," as Morris K. Jessup Professor of Practical Theology at Union Theological Seminary, gives us additional insight into his theory of preaching, especially as it relates to the relationship between biblical criticism and preaching. Relevant to our investigation is his critique of the preaching of his day, which need not go unnoticed, for his abiding words are put forth with pastoral candor: "As one listens to our modern, liberal preaching, how lamentably inadequate it is! Its message too often is thinly contemporary; much of its truth sprang up last night like Jonah's gourd and will as quickly wither again. Its pronouncements, for all their cleverness and altruism, sound like happy ideas that lately popped into the preacher's head. It reminds one of nothing so much as a shallow, surface pool, representative only of the rain that fell yesterday."[4] A keen listener, Fosdick observed that the sermons of his liberal contemporaries were superficial, missing a vital element that makes for excellence in preaching. Their sermons were the consequence of indiscipline in study, inadequate sermon preparation, and incognizance regarding the immediate individual needs and social problems of listeners.

A satiated witness to a Fosdick sermon once related the spiritual nourishment she and her friends received from his preaching: "We [young women] have to go where there is food if we would be fed—That's why we stood in the 'Bread Line'—to get bread, and we got it. And the best part of it is, that we have eaten it, and no one can take it from us."[5] Hungry souls yearning for spiritual nourishment are not satisfied with substance-free

---

4. Harry Emerson Fosdick's inaugural address at Union Theological Seminary, "A Modern Preacher's Problem in His Use of the Scriptures," September 30, 1915.

5. Miller, *Fosdick*, 97.

sermons. Such sermons do not provide the necessary spiritual nutrients to feed the troubled souls occupying our churches. No hungry soul who attends a scheduled church banquet expects not to eat. Of course not. In Fosdick's view, the preachers of his day were not committed to providing expectant worshippers with excellence in preaching through diligent preparation practices. As a matter of fact, no preaching method is worthwhile if the preacher is not willing to work hard and study long.

Published in 1952, Fosdick's autobiography provides insights into the development of his life-situation preaching. Recollecting his preaching ministry at Montclair, Fosdick confessed that he was "an ignoramus about the effective preparation of a sermon."[6] He compared his experience to "a boy thrown into deep water and told to swim when he does not know how."[7] His critique of his seminary's lectures in homiletics is that, first, they lacked relevance to actual experience, and, second, the information was soon forgotten because it was not implemented in practice. What saved Fosdick, in his own assessment, was his training in public speaking:

> My greater difficulty during my years at Montclair was not with others but with myself. I did not know how to preach. Doubtless part of the trouble was due to my still unsteady nerves, but much of it was still downright ignorance of how to tackle the preparation of a sermon. What saved me, I suspect, was the fact that I had been trained to stand up and talk in public, so that, however little I had to say, I could at least say it.[8]

The effective preparation of a sermon proved inordinately difficult for Fosdick. The process of composing meaningful and purposeful sermons was tortuously painful for young Fosdick, as he revealed in his autobiography: "I recall vividly the tormented weeks I spent during the first year and more in Montclair, often distraught myself and fairly driving my wife to distraction, trying to prepare sermons that would be worth preaching."[9] Frustrated and discontented with the prevailing expository and topical sermons, which we have already discussed, Fosdick found himself in a stalemate. He dared not continue his rote, nor give up the pastorate. The gist of the problem was that the essence of what he wanted to say was at odds with the traditional method of sermon preparation and the prevailing

---

6. Fosdick, *Autobiography*, 83.
7. Ibid.
8. Ibid.
9. Ibid., 84.

approaches to preaching. As a result, a new approach to preaching was a nonnegotiable desideratum for the struggling young preacher.

Fosdick believed that effective preaching should be practical, substantive, relevant and actionable; and, above all, it should address life situations with which people are having difficulty. On his journey to effective preaching, Fosdick thought through the purpose of a sermon and concluded: "People come to church on Sunday with every kind of personal difficulty and problem flesh is heir to. A sermon was meant to meet such needs; it should be personal counseling on a group scale."[10] He believed that the sermon should have a practical objective—it should meet the needs of people. To do this, Fosdick ingeniously incorporated personal counseling into pastoral ministry in order to keenly understand and intelligently address practical matters regarding people's problems through life-situation preaching. Personal counseling was the medium through which he gleaned insight ("clairvoyance" as he called it) into human nature: "If one had clairvoyance, one would know the sins and shames, the anxieties and doubts, the griefs and disillusionments, that filled the pews, and could by God's grace bring the saving truths of the gospel to bear on them as creatively as though he were speaking to a single person. That was the place to start—with the real problems of the people. That was a sermon's specialty, which made it a sermon, not an essay or a lecture.[11] The person, the individual, although in a crowd, was the object of Fosdick's approach to preaching. His silent prayer each Sunday was for the individual: "O God, some one person here needs what I am going to say. Help me to reach him!"[12]

Intellectually frustrated with the topical and expository methods, Fosdick started his sermons with listeners real problems. He was convinced that the Gospel should be brought to bear on some problem that afflicted people. A sermon, as he saw it, was designed to meet such needs. In this sense he posits: "Every sermon should have for its main business the head-on constructive meeting of some problem which was puzzling minds, burdening conscience, distracting lives, and no sermon which so met a real human difficulty, with light to throw on it and help to win a victory over it, could possibly be futile."[13] Although this statement comes from Fosdick's autobiography, it is a restatement from an article he wrote

10. Ibid., 94.
11. Ibid.
12. Ibid., 100.
13. Ibid.

for *Harper's Magazine* in 1928. In his homiletical experimentation, Fosdick discovered that the congregation was responding to his preaching because he was handling a subject of vital interest to them. A preacher is "functioning," according to Fosdick, if the preacher is helping folk to solve their real problems. "Any preacher who, with even moderate skill, is thus helping folk to solve their real problems is functioning. He never will lack an audience. He may have little learning or eloquence but he is doing the one thing that is a preacher's special business. He is delivering the goods which the community has a right to expect from the pulpit."[14] The efficacy of the Fosdickian life-situation approach lies in the crucial truth that Fosdick was genuinely concerned with helping people solve their problems.

In light of this, it is not surprising that Fosdick started his sermons with "life situations," as his preaching was a person-centered undertaking. In part, this means that the person and her attendant problems provided the content for his preaching. A sermon was not merely a discussion on some topic; it should create in the congregation the thing the preacher is talking about. What does Fosdick mean by this? He explains:

> My own major difficulty sprang from the fact that starting a sermon with a problem, however vital and urgent, suggests a discussion, a dissertation, a treatise. A sermon, however, is more than that. The preacher's business is not merely to discuss repentance but to persuade people to repent; not merely debate the meaning and possibility of Christian faith, but to produce Christian faith in the lives of his listeners; not merely to talk about the available power of God to bring victory over trouble and temptation, but to send people out from their worship on Sunday with victory in their possession.[15]

Thus, the sermon should do something significant and tangible in the lives of listeners. It should achieve results; meet real needs; and bring about the transformation of human personality from a troubled listener to a victorious believer. Fosdick's experimentation with life-situation preaching became exhilarating. He discovered that preaching need not fail to make a transforming difference in someone's life if the preacher is dealing with the "profoundest concerns of personality, with incalculable possibilities dependent on what is said that day."[16] Fosdick was convinced that preaching

---

14. Ibid., 95.
15. Ibid., 98.
16. Ibid., 100.

should speak to the deepest problems and communicate how the gospel can be brought to bear on those problems to bring about spiritual transformation and rejuvenation.

His approach to preaching does not presuppose expertise in the art of preaching. On the contrary, it is universally applicable to preachers of modest ability. Fosdick remarked that sermons were uninteresting, inconsequential, and disconnected from the congregation; there was nothing of lasting value in the sermons he listened to. His critique of the mediocre sermon is worth noting: "One obvious trouble with the mediocre sermon, even when harmless, is that it is uninteresting. It does not matter. It could as well be left unsaid. It produces this effect of emptiness and futility largely because it establishes no connection with the real interests of the congregation."[17] However well intended the sermon, however genuine the preacher, however thorough the method, if the preacher takes for granted the thinking and concerns of people, the preacher is not functioning. To this end, he writes bluntly: "It is pathetic to observe the number of preachers who commonly on Sunday speak religious pieces in the pulpit, utterly failing to establish real contact with the thinking or practical interests of their auditors."[18] In his observation, the preachers of his day were concerned with religious ideas that were of little concern to people's thinking and living. Vital needs and deep concerns were unaddressed sermonically. Fosdick's vocabulary reveals his disdain for such sermons when he uses uncharitable words ("pathetic" and "unnecessary") to describe ineffective preachers who fail to establish a vital connection with listeners because their homiletical gauge did not accurately display the interests and concerns of the congregation.

Fosdick notes further that all things being equal (a capable preacher, an appropriate text, and a well-chosen and well-developed sermon), the effect of a sermon is contingent upon the preacher's ability to make something transformative happen in people's lives. Pointedly, he said: "The subject was well chosen and well developed, but for all that, nothing happened. The effect was flat. So far as the sermon was concerned, the congregation might as well have stayed home."[19] In stern criticism of the topical and expository methods, Fosdick notes what he sees as the limitations of these methods and their unfortunate consequences: "The reason for this [ineffectiveness

17. Fosdick, "What Is the Matter With Preaching?," 28.
18. Ibid.
19. Ibid., 33.

Life-Situation Preaching for African-Americans

of the sermon] can commonly be traced to one cause: the preacher started his sermon at the wrong end. He made it the exposition of a text or the elucidation of a subject instead of a well-planned endeavor to help solve some concrete problems in the individual lives before him."[20] Whatever the case, the preacher's method of preparation has dire consequences for the composition and preaching of a sermon.

The problem that Fosdick observes is not that the preacher lacks intelligence or character but rather the preacher's method is flawed. A flawed method only produces flawed sermons, as it corrupts the integrity of the sermon composition process, thereby producing sermons that are of little to no interest to listeners. It is not an exaggeration to say that for Fosdick everything comes down to method—the preacher's approach to sermon composition and preaching. As he saw it, the problem with flawed preaching was threefold. First, the preacher tends to lack a worthwhile method of sermon preparation; second, the training received in seminary often lacks a practical element that enables the preacher to connect with listeners; and third, the preacher fails to see clearly the aim of the sermon. Fosdick taught that the only justifiable aim of the sermon is to help people solve their problems. Period.

Thus, for Fosdick, an interesting sermon is one that helps people in a practical way to understand and overcome their problems. The preacher arouses the congregation's interest when the sermon is a practical affair in which the preacher is "handling a subject they are puzzled about, or way of living they have dangerously experimented with, or an experience that has bewildered them, or an ideal they have been trying to make real, or a need they have not known how to meet."[21] When the preacher fails to address a practical concern or fails to connect with the people, the preacher's earnest endeavor amounts to a futile homiletical exercise. If it is true, as Fosdick has said, that people are interested only in themselves, their own problems, and the way to solve their problems, then it is also true that any approach to ministry that takes seriously the needs and interest of people is going attract the listener's attention.

As noted previously, the final test of a sermon's effectiveness for Fosdick was how many individuals sought the preacher for counseling after the preaching event. He addressed the matter explicitly when he said that his "ideal of a sermon is an animated conversation with the audience

20. Ibid.
21. Ibid., 29.

concerning some vital problem of the spiritual life."[22] Effective preaching for Fosdick was an "animated conversation" in which the preacher was able to establish critical contact with the problems and concerns of listeners through vibrant preaching. He advised that "the more a preacher can make his sermon an elevated and animated rendition of the sort of thing he would do for an individual soul, when he was at his best, the better the sermon is likely to be."[23] In this regard the the preacher is not to be concerned with preaching a sermon solely for the purpose of edification or indoctrination, although this can certainly be a part of it, but rather for the sole purpose of helping people solve their real problems.

Gardner Taylor relates that Dr. Paul Scherer once said that preaching is 10 percent genius and 90 percent firm application of the pants to a chair.[24] This is incontestably true in the case of Fosdick. As far as he was concerned, nothing could make preaching easy. He believed that preaching involved "drenching a congregation with one's lifeblood."[25] A consummate craftsman, Fosdick worked hard to produce sermons. In fact, the hallmark of a Fosdick sermon was and is the noticeable mark of sweaty equity. For, indeed, each sermon was the product of intense thinking, extensive research, and long hours. His method of sermon composition took an entire week. In fact, Fosdick worked about sixteen hours every week on a sermon that lasted about one-half hour. He displayed discipline, diligence, creativity, and intelligence in sermon composition. He worked through various parts of his sermon Monday through Thursday, finishing the final manuscript on Friday noon. On Saturday mornings, he rethought the matter as if his congregation were visibly before his eyes, meticulously editing and rewording his manuscript. Invariably, Fosdick's sermon was ready for the pulpit by noontime Saturday. What we learn from Fosdick is that no method will produce the desired results of effective preaching if a preacher is unwilling to surrender self to systematic reading, discipline in writing, and critical theological reflection. The time spent in study will pay dividends during sermon delivery. Having established a fundamental grounding in Fosdick's theory of preaching, I now turn to the mechanics of his approach.

---

22. Fosdick, "Animated Conversation," 47.
23. Ibid., 48.
24. Taylor, "Building A Sermon," 172.
25. Fosdick, "What Is The Matter With Preaching?," 30.

Life-Situation Preaching for African-Americans

Mechanics of Fosdick's Life-Situation Preaching

Previously it was noted that in 1928 Fosdick published an article entitled "How I Prepare My Sermons" in *Harper's Magazine*.[26] This article explicates his approach to the preparation of a sermon. Foremost for Fosdick was the practical usefulness of a sermon. The thesis of "How I Prepare My Sermons" is that every sermon's central motive should be the achievement of some definite objective; that is to say, every sermon should have a specific intent or aim. Although brief, the article provides keen insight into Fosdick's preparation of a sermon, delivery, and techniques.

Fosdick identifies two factors involved in the origin of a sermon—a definite objective (purpose of the sermon) and relevant truth (an implement or resource to serve a definite intent). As regards the former, Fosdick's approach to the preparation of a sermon began with intense mentation regarding what he hoped the sermon would achieve once preached. First, he brainstormed what he hoped to achieve in a sermon (the aim) and what he hoped the sermon would achieve in people's lives (the results). In "Animated Conversation," Fosdick explains this process clearly: "No sermon seems to me to get well under way until I have clearly in mind some difficulty that people are facing, some question that they are asking, some sin they are committing, some possibility they are missing, some confused thinking they are doing, so that I have before me rather a goal toward which I aim than simply a subject or a text from which I talk."[27]

Having a clear picture of the sermon's objective was the first critical step for Fosdick. He further clarified the point when he wrote: "It may be to help individuals in facing some personal problem, or the answering of a puzzling question in theology, or the persuasion of tempted souls to abandon some popular sin, or the confrontation of some public evil with the Christian ethic, or the winning of wavering minds and consciences to a definite decision for Christ, but I, for one, cannot start a sermon until I clearly see what I propose to get done on Sunday morning."[28] The object of Fosdick's sermon always involved a subject. Indeed, an analysis of listeners' needs during personal consultation provided a wealth of information and new ideas for a sermon. The subject of Fosdick's life-situation sermon is derived from congregational needs. In this regard, Linn notes: "Thus the

---

26. Fosdick, "Prepare My Sermons."
27. Fosdick, "Animated Conversation," 47.
28. Fosdick, "Prepare My Sermons," 43.

Fosdick's Preaching Ministry

sermon subject is not merely the whim of the preacher, nor a late item from the newspaper, nor an exposition of a Bible passage, but is the satisfaction of some personal need of one or more of the congregation."[29] Fosdick was in touch with the way in which the forces of life—individual, social, economic, and international—affected individuals.

In *On Being a Real Person*, Fosdick notes that people faced fears, confusions, sins, prejudices, hates, loves, successes, doubts, sorrows, failures, despair, conflicts, sicknesses, diseases, and inferiorities.[30] Copious ideas emanate from such aspects of life. "The selection of this problem at the beginning," explains Linn, "is of utmost importance because it becomes the goal to which he must aim."[31] Fosdick's choice of subject was something that was troubling to the vast majority of his listeners, as noted earlier.

Second, after the selection of an object and a subject, Fosdick searched for a relevant truth, turning to the Bible invariably. Sometimes a single passage would suffice; other times, multiple passages. The biblical passages were explained in a highly specialized manner that undergirded the sermon. Such passages were relevant to the aim of the sermon or meant to drive home the purpose of the sermon. That is to say, the relevant truth reinforced the aim of the sermon. "The preacher does not tell all that he knows . . . but he carefully uses its relevant meaning to throw light on the specific purpose."[32] The reason for finding and putting forward a relevant truth in the first place is, in Fosdick's words, "to drop the truth, like a pile driver, ramming home the impact to achieve a definite result."[33] The relevant truth is a concrete and universally accepted truth that helps the sermon to achieve its purpose.

Third, after determining the definite objective and relevant truth, Fosdick practiced free association of ideas, a phrase borrowed from psychology. He wrote down any idea that was directly or indirectly relevant to his sermon. Fosdick expounds on this point:

> At this stage I do not consider how the sermon will begin or end or what its structure is going to be. I give free gangway to my mind

---

29. Linn, *Preaching as Counseling*, 27. Some of the general sources of subjects for preaching include the needs of listeners, written correspondence such as a personal letter, knowledge of psychology, and reading general literature (28–30).

30. Fosdick, *Real Person*, 3.

31. Linn, *Preaching as Counseling*, 28.

32. Ibid., 67.

33. Fosdick, "Prepare My Sermons," 43.

and let it pick up anything within the scope of the sermon's object and subject which it may chance to light upon. If an idea is only a vague intimation with no development or application evident, I do not labor it. If an idea branches out into consecutive suggestions, I briefly note them. I observe no logical continuity in accepting any suggestion that may come but jot it down. This process may go on for hours—one awakening another and all of them unorganized jumble and potpourri, without order or logical connection; but, not infrequently, when this stage is finished, I have the basic material, the loose bricks, with which the sermon will be built.[34]

As one can see, Fosdick gave his mind complete freedom to consider any idea that traversed his mental highway. Subsequent to determining the definite objective and relevant truth and brainstorming, Fosdick worked on the organization of his sermon. This was a creative process. Fosdick asked four specific research questions to help him communicate the matter at hand. A quick survey of the research questions suggests four different areas of inquiry, such as literature, personal counseling, the Bible, and personal experience. The questions are as follow:

1. What have I ever read in general literature—biography, history, novels, poetry—that throws light upon my theme?

2. What have I ever run upon in personal counseling that illustrates the human need with which I am dealing and the resources to meet it?

3. Where, beyond the passages I have already thought of, does the Bible—that vast storehouse of experience—illumine the sermon's problem and the way to treat it?

4. What, in my own personal experience, has this intimately meant to me, and what—honest to goodness!—does it really mean now in my own life?[35]

Once researched, the answers provide the structural outline of the sermon. The sermon's structure emerged from the research. Of course, none of his sermons developed in the same way. Each was different. Fosdick arranged his thoughts psychologically, not logically. This is not to say that he was inclined to writing illogical sermons. Certainly not! The rationale for this structure is simple. The preacher, he wrote, "is after his audience to create a change in them, and therefore his primary endeavor must be to

34. Ibid.
35. Ibid., 44.

arrange his thought in a psychological fashion, so that he may start where they are in their thinking . . ."[36]

As it relates to the psychological arrangement of the sermon, the practical application was foremost, as it could make or break a sermon. Fosdick wrote: "I often find that this contrast between a merely logical and a vitally psychological arrangement of thought can make or unmake a sermon."[37] When the psychological outline did not emerge, Fosdick commenced writing until the outline became clear. This process was tedious at times, but he developed the discipline to see it through.

Previously we saw that it was not unusual for Fosdick to spend sixteen to twenty hours each week composing his sermons. He noted that sometimes the entire organization of the sermon was clear; other times he only saw where to begin; other times he started with the relevant truth; other times, he began with an illustration or the conclusion. Suffice it to say that the sermon's structure was a creative process that emerged while thinking, reading, and writing. Writing was an important part of sermon composition for Fosdick. Of course, when writing, one need not always begin at the beginning or even in the middle; one can actually begin at the end, as many a writer-preacher does. But with persistence and perseverance all of the parts eventually begin to come together. So Fosdick's experience is not all that unusual, but it is good to know what he sometimes experienced when writing the sermon.

As regards preaching and writing, the two practices have an interdependent relationship in Fosdick's approach. In fact, it was inconceivable to him for a preacher to preach without having written out a manuscript in full: "I do not see how a man can preach without writing. I always have thought with my pen in hand. My preaching naturally began to turn into books."[38] Every sermon preached by Fosdick was written in full by hand. In his critical observation of preachers who do not write, Fosdick noticed "monotonous style, a limited vocabulary with few synonyms, repetitious ruts of thought, and finally a quick change of pastorate to find a congregation unfamiliar with the preacher's now well-worn clichés."[39]

Writing sermons has it benefits, to be sure. Writing, explains Fosdick, "forces careful consideration of phraseology, makes the preacher weigh his

---

36. Fosdick, "Prepare My Sermons," 43.
37. Crocker, "Rhetorical Theory," 233–34.
38. Fosdick, *Autobiography*, 89.
39. Fosdick, "Prepare My Sermons," 44.

Life-Situation Preaching for African-Americans

words, compels him to reread what he has written and criticize it without mercy, constrains him to clear up obscurities in thought and language, begets discontent with repetitious mannerisms, and allows the preacher, before he mounts the pulpit, to listen, as it were, to his own sermon as a whole and judge whether it would hit his nail on the head were he an auditor."[40] Hence, writing is indispensable to effective preaching. As one writer put it, "After the success of his early books, he must have realized he could reach two audiences. With one compositional effort, he concomitantly addressed the spiritual needs of his immediate listeners and reached his reading public."[41] Suffice it to say, Fosdick encouraged the preachers of his day to write their manuscripts in full to avoid the aforementioned pitfalls.

Writing a sermon for listeners can be a challenging undertaking, as preaching from a manuscript can be a monotonous and somnolent experience for the congregation, especially if the preacher lacks enthusiasm and controlled animation. To this, Fosdick responded, "No sermon need be so written that it lacks spontaneity."[42] Fosdick overcame this problem by learning to write for listeners and not readers. He had a gift for writing conversational-styled sermons. When done well, the listeners, Fosdick notes, will neither know nor care that the preacher reads from a manuscript. As Halford R. Ryan observed: "The nexus of Harry Emerson Fosdick's career was his ability to write for preaching and to preach in writing."[43] Fosdick maintained a writing-for-speaking routine throughout his professional ministry, Ryan notes. Writing for listeners necessitates a different approach to the composition of a sermon. Fosdick discovered that he could preach from a manuscript as though he were not reading but talking. Moreover, he discovered that he could do so with "just as much freedom, spontaneity, colloquial directness, and person-to-person impact as though no manuscript were on the pulpit."[44]

Fosdick's direct, colloquial discourse used in his sermons and lectures presupposed listeners and envisioned a particular group to whom he

40. Ibid., 44–45.
41. Ryan, *Persuasive Preacher*, 8.
42. Ibid., 45.
43. Ibid., 7.
44. Fosdick, "How I Prepare My Sermons," 45. Charles J. Adams, senior pastor at Hartford Memorial Baptist Church in Detroit, is a well-known and respected black preacher who preaches well from a manuscript. None who heard him preach could come away thinking that he was anything less than a consummate artist in preaching from a manuscript.

spoke. He used his imagination in the composition of a sermon. That is, as he composed his sermon, he imagined the specific type of person whose mind and conscience he proposed to reach and wrote as though the two of them were face-to-face. The upshot, according to Fosdick, "ought to be one of talk—plain, straightforward, illuminating, helpful talk—between the preacher and his congregation."[45] Linn notes two crucial factors of Fosdick's conversational-styled writing. He says, first, the sermon must be written in an oral style that is clear, and, second, the preacher must skillfully introduce insight and experience into the speaking environment so he can adapt the sermon to the listeners' attitudes and reactions.[46]

Fosdick eschewed pulpit theatrics. For him, the sermon was to be conversational in tone and free of "all manner of pulpit tricks designed merely to do stunts with a congregation."[47] His biographer described his pulpit mannerisms vividly: "He mounted the pulpit not slouchingly, but soldierly. His posture in the pulpit was erect, but not awkwardly stiff, the feet separated, the right slightly in advance of the left. The gestures were few and restrained."[48] The sermon, an "animated conversation," was a helpful talk between the preacher and the congregation, just as the preacher would talk, plainly, to an individual. To achieve maximum effect, Fosdick introduced opposing personalities in his preaching, thus creating a dialogue as opposed to a monologue. One author named this tactic "adversative sermonizing."[49] Fosdick employed such phrases as "to point out a contrast" and "let us consider a contrary thought" to introduce opposing objections. He did this to address "objections, difficulties, and contradictory experiences that would occur to the person listening to any discourse."[50]

Linn noted that Fosdick's approach followed a discernable, although not uniform, organizational structure: (1) choose a problem, (2) define the specific purpose, (3) choose the relevant truth, (4) free association of ideas, (5) ask exploratory questions, (6) ask radical questions, (7) write the opening section, (8) phrase the specific purpose and the relevant truth to achieve it, (9) write the main points, (10) write the sermon in full, (11) revise the

---

45. Fosdick, "Animated Conversation," 48.
46. Linn, *Preaching as Counseling*, 147.
47. Fosdick, "Animated Conversation," 48.
48. Miller, *Fosdick*, 370.
49. See Ryan, "A Preacher Preaching," 58.
50. Ibid., 49.

manuscript. Often times, these steps overlapped.[51] Linn has done a marvelous job of articulating the mechanics of Fosdick's approach to preaching.[52] What is helpful for our purpose is Linn's contention that "the need of the listener affects nearly everything about preaching—method, content, organization, language, and delivery."[53] Thus, there is no aspect of the preparation of a life-situation sermon that is untouched by the listener's needs. Having explored Fosdick's theory of preaching and the mechanics of his life-situation preaching, it is important to consider some of the strengths and weaknesses of his preaching model, which is the subject of chapter 4.

---

51. Linn, *Preaching as Counseling*, 72–73.
52. Ibid., 27.
53. Ibid.

4

Strengths and Weaknesses of Fosdick's Life-Situation Preaching

Strengths of Fosdick's Life-Situation Preaching

Preaching is central in Protestantism. It is the medium through which the gospel is proclaimed, and salvation is achieved. However foolish or flippant one's views on preaching, the fact remains that it is the constitutive act of the church. Paul speaks emphatically to this point in his contention that God decisively chose preaching to achieve God's salvific purpose: "For since, in the wisdom of God, the world did not know God through wisdom, God decided, through the foolishness of our proclamation, to save those who believe" (1 Cor 1:21). Prior to exploring the weaknesses and strengths of Fosdick's life-situation preaching, it is important to have a working definition of preaching that is nearly consistent across so-called mainline churches. This is a sort of homiletical measuring stick, if you will, for Fosdick's life-situation preaching.

In *Power in the Pulpit*, Jerry Vines and Jim Shaddix define preaching as "the oral communication of biblical truth by the Holy Spirit through a human personality to a given audience with the intent of enabling a positive response."[1] Preaching in this sense has a specific activity (oral communication), a specific message (biblical truth), a specific medium (Holy

---

1. Vines and Shaddix, *Power in the Pulpit*, 27.

Life-Situation Preaching for African-Americans

Spirit), a specific recipient (the audience), and a specific motive (positive response from the people). If this definition has even the slightest merit, then Fosdick's life-situation preaching should be used cautiously and prudently, because it, similar to any homiletical method, has weaknesses.

Although critics argue that Fosdick's life-situation preaching deemphasizes the importance of the Bible as a community book; fails to acknowledge the role of the Holy Spirit in sermon preparation and preaching; and is disconnected from the doctrine of the church, his approach to preaching still has some significant strengths. Young preachers and novice preachers new to ministry or discontent with the prevailing approaches to preaching can learn from Fosdick's life-situation preaching. Given that Fosdick's life-situation preaching has been addressed, this section will briefly highlight some of its strengths.

The obvious advantage of life-situation preaching is that it speaks directly to people's needs and attempts to solve their problems. It seeks to touch the deepest layer of existence and to speak to the universality of human experience. At the center of life-situation preaching and everything that the church does is people—people who have unique physical, mental, spiritual, economical, and practical needs, to name a few. Therefore, preaching that addresses people's needs has enduring power and pertinence. Fosdick once said that a sermon should meet the needs of the people who come to church on Sunday with every kind of personal difficulty. The genius of this approach is that the sermon immediately attracts people's attention because the issues addressed through preaching are relevant to listeners' lives. Put another way, the life-situation sermon starts with the needs of the individual because this is the individual's utmost concern; and this approach to preaching has an enduring popularity because it is rooted in, and draws its ingredients from, the lives of people.[2]

First, as we have argued throughout, life-situation preaching at its best takes seriously the personal problems of people. The sermon based on such preaching forces the preacher to plumb the depths of human existence,

---

2. A notable example of life-situation preaching's enduring popularity is the preaching of Joel Scott Osteen. He is an American preacher, televangelist, author, and the Senior Pastor of Lakewood Church, Houston, Texas, the largest Protestant church in the United States. His televised ministry reaches over 7 million viewers weekly and over 20 million viewers monthly in over 100 countries. Five of Osteen's books were named New York Times Best Sellers. Osteen's life-situation preaching does not align with orthodox theology or traditional Christian beliefs. For a fuller account of Osteen's beliefs, see his first published book, *Your Best Life Now*.

Strengths and Weaknesses of Fosdick's Life-Situation Preaching

to take a trek through the inner lives of the congregants, and to face the uncensored human personality in the raw. Superficiality has no place in preaching or counseling. The natural corollary of superficial ministry is superficial preaching and superficial results. A mere concern for people is insufficient. In Fosdick's life-situation preaching, one deals with the profoundest concerns of human personality. Such an approach encourages the preacher to become intimately concerned with personalities and what goes on inside them—the inner dynamics and source of discord. With his approach, the preacher is not just preaching a sermon on a subject. To the contrary, the preacher is attempting to solve people's spiritual problems in order to make them spiritually whole.

Second, Fosdick's life-situation preaching is helpful to young preachers with little or no ministry experience. With this approach to preaching, there is the hope of relevance and purpose even for young preachers or novice preachers with mediocre skills. Moreover, this approach is useful to preachers of all varieties: educated and uneducated, eloquent or ineloquent, young or old, mainline or nondenominational. Regardless of the preacher's credentials, she will have an audience because she is helping people to solve their real problems. She is, in the words of Fosdick, "delivering the goods which the community has a right to expect from the pulpit."[3] This approach is effective because the preacher does not begin the sermon with the preacher's own subjective interests but with some important question, difficult problem, or troubling "life-situation" that the preacher must help his congregation live with or through. Doubtless, young preachers and novice preachers will encounter problems that they feel professionally ill equipped to handle ably. Dealing with such problems is difficult. Preaching on such problems is even more difficult. Life-situation preaching brings people's problems into dialogue with the Bible in order to facilitate healing through the proclamation of the word of God. In the end, young preachers and novice preachers will be "functioning," to use Fosdick's apt phrase, because they are performing a vital task for the church.

Third, Fosdick's life-situation preaching is practical preaching. The life-situation preacher is engaged in a practical endeavor to highlight a problem or felt need, to wrestle with it in the pulpit intelligently and carefully, and to shed light on it with the gospel. This approach encourages the young preacher to conduct an exposition of human personality in order to help people think and live through their real problems. Yes, the mechanics

3. Fosdick, *Autobiography*, 95.

are important. What is most important, however, is that the preacher understands and is able to offer a practical solution to the perplexing problems of listeners. A distinctive feature of Fosdick's preaching that is often overlooked is its insistence on a practical result, which gives the sermon its purpose and direction.

Another advantage of life-situation preaching noted by Fosdick is its emphasis on preaching that produces transformation of its listeners. With respect to this advantage, Fosdick remarked: "It [life-situation preaching] actually brings to pass in the lives of the congregation the thing it talks about. So, to tackle the problem of joy so that the whole congregation goes out more joyful than it came in—that is the mark of a genuine sermon."[4] Fosdick's preaching was an appeal for a decision. One may credit this to his seminary speech professor, Francis Carmody, a Roman Catholic layman with a legal background. He taught at Union Theological Seminary from 1903 to 1928. He trained his students to preach for a verdict, to marshal their arguments, and to give their evidence tellingly.[5] This is quite different from merely preaching about joy. Joy is to be produced in the lives of the congregation. The sermon, Carmody instructed, must be compellingly delivered so as to convince listeners to act or live in a certain way.

Fosdick's life-situation preaching requires clairvoyance into the people's thinking. This point is unequivocally clear in his thought. So much so, he argues that "any man who lacks this [clairvoyance] has no business to preach anyway."[6] Explanatorily, he said: "A preacher, even in his youth, gifted with some clear convictions about the meaning of personal and social life at their best can approach in a straightforward fashion the questions which people are asking, the problems they are facing, and the experiences that perplex them in private life or social situations."[7] Personal counseling deepens the preacher's clairvoyance by teaching the preacher about human nature. The preacher gains an invaluable insight into the lives of folks. Not abstract knowledge that is the result of limited personal experiences or

4. Fosdick, "What Is the Matter with Preaching?," 37.

5. Coffin, *Union Theological Seminary*, 72. Carmody was once a professor at the University of Notre Dame. He also taught at the Law School of Fordham University. Fosdick's colloquial-styled written sermons owe their facility of delivery to Carmody. Coffin noted that Carmody "could take a monotonous voice and get variety into it" (ibid.). "Without making men theatrical," Coffin continued, "he could render them much more effective in speaking what they had written" (ibid.).

6. Fosdick, *Autobiography*, 97.

7. Fosdick, "The Christian Ministry," 63.

Strengths and Weaknesses of Fosdick's Life-Situation Preaching

untested hypotheses, but rather first-hand knowledge of hurt, pain, loss, distress, despair and the like. One preacher put it in explicit terms when he said that the "great *sine qua non* of effective preaching is insight into life; not simply knowledge of the facts of life, but insight into the nature of life."[8] Young men and women can gain such insights into preaching through a direct encounter with human nature and personality through personal counseling, which will undoubtedly help to develop personal and professional relationships with members, especially those who are facing difficult problems. Unbreakable bonds are forged between the pastor and the help-seeker in the crucible of personal crises.

As discussed in chapter 2, personal counseling gradually led Fosdick to life-situation preaching, which, in his own words, made preaching "an exciting adventure."[9] In Fosdick's thought, the young preacher who practices personal counseling is going to find that his or her sermons, in content and form, are profoundly affected. The relationship between personal counseling and preaching is one of interdependence. This interactional process contributes to the preacher's ability to compose and preach relevant and purposeful sermons. Fosdick believed that the right kind of preacher is coerced to become a personal counselor, and the right kind of personal counselor gains some of the most necessary ingredients of preaching.[10]

As we saw earlier, the ultimate test of a sermon for Fosdick is the number of people who seek the preacher's counsel after the sermon. Preachers do well to remember that personal counseling can and does inform preaching, but, if not handled judiciously, can have disastrous consequences. Fosdick likened personal counseling to a marriage in that it is not to be entered into unadvisedly or lightly.[11] His aim was to help people, especially young people. Sympathetic to young men and women entering Christian ministry, Fosdick hoped to help them avoid and overcome the malaise associated with the preaching ministry. He desired to share his knowledge and years of experience with young people in order to help them navigate the turbulent waves of ministry. The discussion on the strengths of Fosdick's life-situation preaching has been intentionally brief, as the benefits of this method are advanced throughout this book. The reader will benefit from

---

8. Ruopp, "Life Situation Preaching," 116–17.
9. Fosdick, *Autobiography*, 93.
10. Fosdick, "Personal Counseling and Preaching," 51.
11. Fosdick, *Real Person*, xiii.

thorough discussion on the precise reasons that many preachers debunk this preaching method, which is the subject of the next section.

Weaknesses of Fosdick's Life-Situation Preaching

Fosdick once presented his homiletical approach to a group of experienced ministers and received some critical feedback. Many of them, for various reasons, were unsuccessful in their use of his method. One objection from the group was that the experimenters overstated their opposing argument and then failed to answer the objections. They misused or overused adversative sermonizing. The preachers expended too much time on counter-arguments to the extent that the sermon concluded with those arguments and not the practical solution. Another objection was that the preachers were so practical in their thinking about some definite problem that they became trivial, thereby failing to bring the gospel to bear on the issue. These preachers failed to respond to the felt needs of their people with the power of the gospel, leaving the congregation without a biblical response to their human problems. An additional objection was that the preachers were so anxious to deal with felt needs in the congregation that they forgot to arouse listeners' consciousness regarding the unfelt but real needs. Thus, the preachers dealt with the felt needs unintelligently and unskillfully in the sermon.

Fosdick attributes such objections not to the method, but rather to the preachers' unskilled handling of it. Any method, in his view, could be wrecked if the preacher lacked skill. This method, Fosdick wrote, "can be offensively personal, argumentatively unconvincing, practically trivial, and narrowed to the conscious needs of mediocre people."[12] The danger that he saw most clearly was that the word "problem" suggested merely a debate and the presentation of helpful ideas. A sermon that was merely a discussion was ineffective in his eyes. Hence, preachers who used this method to discuss a problem with no biblical insights or relevant truths were using it inefficaciously.

Linn also speaks to this matter in a helpful way. He points to five temptations of preachers that can lead to an unskilled handling of life-situation preaching. He cautions that such temptations can ruin any homiletical method. First, the preacher can embarrass listeners. If the preacher discloses a notable experience or confidential information during the sermon,

---

12. Fosdick, "What Is the Matter with Preaching?," 36.

Strengths and Weaknesses of Fosdick's Life-Situation Preaching

listeners could perceive it as a breach of confidential communication, as though the preacher is publicly disclosing a congregant's personal business. Second, the preacher can overlook the needs of listeners. In haste to find the problem that is troubling most folks, the preacher can unintentionally overlook a listener's important problem and fail to address it from the pulpit, thereby leaving the listener wondering when the preacher is going to say something relevant to her problem.

Third, the preacher can overstate objections, expending so much pulpit time trying to answer objections that the preacher fails to do anything else in the sermon. Such an experience can have disappointing, even disastrous results. Fourth, the preacher may slant the sermon or preach on a subject *ad nauseam*, becoming narrow in preaching, speaking to specific problems or issues of groups at the expense of reaching the entire congregation. Fifth, the preacher can fail to apply the gospel to the problem, thus failing to communicate its redeeming quality.

The weaknesses here noted are by proponents of life-situation preaching—proponents who are aware of the disastrous consequences of using life-situation preaching unskillfully. Scholars and preachers alike take issue with life-situation preaching because it deemphasizes the importance of the Bible; fails to acknowledge the role of the Holy Spirit in sermon preparation and preaching; it is disconnected from the doctrine of the church; and it does not take into consideration the life situations of nonwhite listeners. Each of these criticisms will now be examined in more detail.

The first criticism of Fosdick's life-situation preaching is that it deemphasizes the importance of the Bible, although Fosdick, as noted, would disagree. Critics argue that there is no concrete connection to Scripture in much of life-situation preaching. In Fosdick's preaching, generally speaking, the Bible is used as a resource and not the source of the message, according to his critics. Of course, this is not true for all of his sermons. One author highlights the ambiguity of Fosdick's preaching when he said that it is neither biblical nor unbiblical. He illustrates the dilemma, saying: "Fosdick's life-situation preaching is not necessarily unbiblical preaching even though it begins theoretically with a problem rather than a text, but, on the other hand, it is not necessarily biblical or bound in principle to use a text for the solution to the situation . . ."[13] For the Fosdick critic, the problem is that his preaching is biblically indistinguishable. The Bible, they argue, should be foremost and salient in preaching, since it is the community's

---

13. Beverly, *Fosdick's Predigtweise*, 83.

Life-Situation Preaching for African-Americans

book and the source and foundation of the Christian message. Biblical writers believed that the Bible is the God-breathed word of God. The writer of the Gospel of John recorded as much when he explained: "In the beginning was the Word [*logos*], and the Word was with God, and the Word was God" (1:1). Christian preaching is, or at least should be, steeped in biblical truth, i.e., the word of God. John Killinger observed as much in his theory of preaching: "The greatest preachers have always been lovers of the Bible. Those who have based their preaching on other texts—on the poets, current events, the media, their own opinions—have passed quickly from the scene, as though their ministries were established in quicksand."[14] Hence preaching that fails to take seriously the word of God is situated on precarious ground.

As a result of a long systematic self-study, Fosdick published *A Guide to Understanding the Bible*, in which he traces the development of six major themes—God, man, right and wrong, suffering, fellowship with God, and immortality—using the liberal approach to the Bible. What Fosdick's study reveals is that he, although liberal in his interpretation, was committed to studying the Bible, and that he believed in the "central ideas" of the Bible.[15] Be that as it may, Fosdick's critics argue that his life-situation preaching is not rooted in the symbolism, images, themes, and narratives of the Bible, but rather in human problems. Preaching that is not rooted in the Bible is like "cut flowers that will fade before the evening comes."[16]

The Bible is the book that unites Christians of various denominations; the common denominator in the spiritual and religious life of the church. Our understanding of Christianity originates in and is derived from the Bible. As the universal tool for Christian problems, the Bible touches nearly all aspects of life, either directly or indirectly. Killinger counsels wisely in his summation of the importance of the Bible: "It is simply that the Bible is a book about life, and all-important subjects, regardless of how modern or technical, are reducible to matters of life and how it should be lived."[17] Thus, for Killinger, the Bible speaks to life and addresses life's problems, for it is an inexhaustible resource.

In *Integrative Preaching*, William Willimon observes that "Fosdick's life-situation preaching used the Bible as a secondary appendage to a

---

14. Killinger, *Preaching*, 13.
15. Fosdick, *Understanding the Bible*, xiii–xv.
16. Killinger, *Preaching*, 14.
17. Ibid., 15.

Strengths and Weaknesses of Fosdick's Life-Situation Preaching

sermon taking its cue from life rather than from the text, its problem-solving approach, and so on."[18] To be clear, Willimon's critique of Fosdick is that he used the Bible as a reference in his presentation of a "relevant truth," and not as the ground from which truth springs. Willimon argues that the Bible is not supplemental material; rather, it is the source of the preacher's message, and the substance and content of Christian preaching. Willimon notes further that the Bible is a historically situated and contextualized book, and that "the exegetical and hermeneutical skills a preacher acquires are skills in uncovering and rediscovering the originating and continuing interpretive context for the text."[19] Accordingly, all preaching from the Bible is life-situation preaching in the sense that the preacher speaks to and out of the life situation of the preacher's context and to the life-situation of God's people. Willimon explains his theory of life-situation preaching in this fashion:

> So, in one sense, all preaching from the Bible is "life-situation" preaching—not only preaching to the life-situation of the twentieth century but also preaching out of the life-situation of the centuries before us when God spoke to the life-situation of God's people then. To deny or overlook that context, within the text or within the church today, is to be most unbiblical in overlooking the incarnational, historically contextualized nature of Scripture."[20]

Lest the reader miss the point, Willimon states that preaching from the "Bible" relates the life situation of the text to the life situation of the people. In this sense, life-situation preaching is not unbiblical. It is clear that Willimon disagrees with Fosdick regarding the starting place of a sermon. The place to begin, Willimon maintains, is with the word, the Bible, the tradition and Scripture of the church. Properly understood, a Christian sermon is such because the sermon speaks from a biblical standpoint, not because it addresses the needs of people (although such a sermon should address the relevance of the Bible for people's needs).

So what is the preacher's business in the pulpit? Willimon responds: "In the pulpit we first speak of God's deeds rather humanity's needs. Without God's ceaseless activity and striving after us, we know neither our true needs nor our true selves."[21] Willimon seems to have a single or either-or

18. Willimon, *Integrative Preaching*, 16.
19. Ibid., 17.
20. Ibid.
21. Ibid., 19.

Life-Situation Preaching for African-Americans

approach, rather than a both-and approach. The latter, so it seems, tends to get us closer to truth. Surely there is truth in Fosdick's approach, as there is truth in what Willimon proposes. Fosdick, in contrast to Willimon, starts his sermon on the opposite preaching spectrum, i.e., humanity's needs. Christian preaching is more than good advice; it is the good news of Jesus. It could be said, of course, that whatever else preaching is or is not, it is also good advice, or ought to be. This is the kind of problem that the either-or approach gets one into. In any event, Willimon contends that a Christian sermon ought to be firmly rooted in the Bible.

While in France during WWI as an itinerant preacher with the Y.M.C.A., a sergeant responded to Fosdick's preaching by saying: "I don't know what religion he belongs to, but he has a hell of a lot of sense."[22] The proclamation of the gospel is more than practical wisdom or "good sense." To the contrary, in Willimon's words, "the proclamation of the gospel is that God, in Jesus Christ, has acted and continues to act to save the same humanity that, time and again, has demonstrated it cannot save itself."[23] Preaching, therefore, is not about practical advice or quick fixes to humanity's problems, but rather the eternal truths of the Bible that speaks to God's love for humanity, relating Scripture to human problems. Thus, Willimon affirms "the biblical text as the place to begin a sermon, the place from which the preacher's metaphors, concepts, and truth must be derived."[24]

In a very real sense, then, Willimon makes clear that the preacher's sermon must be derived from biblical theology, as this is the starting place for a right understanding of God, the church, and what God requires of humanity. But in my view, Willimon is only partially right. There is something to Fosdick's starting point in the sermon. That is to say, congregational needs must be weighed properly as it relates to where a preacher begins her sermon. Whether the sermon's focus is on a human need or divine claim is a matter of its importance and relevance to the congregation. There is a paradox here. True, on one hand, a sermon is more than practical wisdom or good sense. Also true, on the other hand, a semon cannot be less than practical wisdom or "good sense."

Homiletician Marvin A. McMickle teaches that every sermon should be focused on a specific message or lesson that is anchored in Scripture. In his estimation, Christian sermons "should speak of Christ, elevate Christ,

---

22. Fosdick, *Autobiography*, 129.
23. Willimon, *Integrative Preaching*, 19.
24. Ibid., 22.

Strengths and Weaknesses of Fosdick's Life-Situation Preaching

and point people to the teachings and blessings that reside in Christ."[25] Similarly, in his study of Fosdick, Beverly says that God is both subject and object of genuine Christian preaching. He criticizes Fosdick's preaching because it is disconnected from the authority of Scripture. Fosdick, to be sure, was more concerned with establishing vital contact with listeners than he was with establishing a connection to Scripture. For Beverly, "Fosdick's theology of preaching, because it severs itself from the authority and hence promises of Scripture concerning preaching, fails to incorporate the promises of God upon which Christian preaching must ever take its stand, and claim for its basis of authority and existence in the life of the Church of Christ."[26]

The problem for Beverly is that the life-situation sermon depends entirely on the preacher for its success. Fosdick was an industrious minister, prolific writer, and extraordinary rhetorician. His words mesmerized his listeners. It is not every day that one hears such beautiful, poetic phrases such as "a volcano was preparing to erupt; one could feel the ominous tremors . . ."[27] Yet, as beautiful a phrase as this is, it pales in comparison to the beauty and power of the gospel. In his letter to the Corinthians, the Apostle Paul acknowledges the temptation to use eloquent speech at the expense of preaching the gospel powerfully and clearly: "For Christ did not send me to baptize but to proclaim the gospel, and not with eloquent wisdom, so that the cross of Christ might not be emptied of its power" (1:17). It would seem as though Fosdick's work ethic supplanted any kind of divine revelation in terms of access to God's veiled truths in the Bible.

One can study any subject studiously or write about any subject prolifically, but that does not mean the finished product was inspired by the Holy Spirit. It is accurate to say, then, that time spent in study is not the same as time spent in God's presence, being guided in preparation by the Holy Spirit. It is not the same, but it is greatly important, just as much as being guided by the Holy Spirit. It is still the case in too much contemporary preaching that the preacher has ostensibly been guided by the Holy Spirit but has failed to spend much time in her study for sermon preparation. Perhaps it is easier to discern when the Holy Spirit is not present than when the Spirit is. One thing is for certain concerning the Holy Spirit: the Spirit brings life, transformation, and renewal to the church.

25. McMickle, *Shaping the Claim*, 5.
26. Beverly, *Fosdick's Predigtweise*, 72.
27. Fosdick, *Autobiography*, 138.

Life-Situation Preaching for African-Americans

Beverly's analysis of Fosdick claims that Fosdick's life-situation preaching failed to relate preaching to the word of God, thus exhibiting a gross failure to understand the importance of the Bible for the art of preaching. In Beverly's view, Fosdick's departure from the Bible represents an attempt to radically alter the Christian message in preaching—"an attempt to define preaching as a message to man from man about himself rather than as an attempt to be faithful exegetically and theologically to the Biblical witness to the Grace of God in Jesus Christ on man's behalf."[28] Matter-of-factly, Beverly states that whenever a Christian sermon loses its distinctive message, its solid biblical base of authority, and its organic connection to Scripture and the tradition of the Church, it ceases to be a sermon. A counterpoint to Beverly's argument is that he misunderstood Fosdick's view on the use of the Bible. Fosdick was preeminently concerned with using the Bible intelligently, unencumbered by Biblicist principles. Fosdick took the Bible seriously, just not literally.

The second criticism of Fosdick's life-situation preaching is that it fails to acknowledge the role of the Holy Spirit in sermon preparation and preaching. In Protestantism, the role of the Holy Spirit is particularly important, as it is constitutive to the church. Sophisticated contemporary preachers, shaped by the presuppositions of the postmodern ethos, do not speak very often about the Holy Spirit. In the case of Fosdick, it is important to remember that he was a liberal preacher, a modernist much in tuned with the scientific discoveries and advances of his day, especially new knowledge in biblical criticism. A veritable modernist, Fosdick rejected the virgin birth as historic fact, repudiated the literal inerrancy of Scripture, and disbelieved the second coming of Jesus Christ.[29] Christianity, for

---

28. Beverly, *Fosdick's Predigtweise*, 81.

29. Liberal Protestantism arose out of a need to relate the Christian faith to the human situation and modern knowledge. In England, Charles Darwin's theory of natural selection (popularly known as the "Darwinian theory of evolution") challenged traditional Christian theology. Liberalism sought to bridge the gap between Christian faith and modern knowledge. The result was that liberals exercised freedom in relation to Christian doctrine and traditional methods of biblical interpretation in order to achieve synthesis. To achieve synthesis, a number of Christian beliefs were abandoned (outdated or mistaken presuppositions) or reinterpreted (in line with cultural norms). Liberalism was a compromise between fundamentalism and the total rejection of the Christian faith. See Alister E. McGrath, *Christian Theology*, 82–84. Regarding Fosdick's belief, Kenneth Cauthen, in *The Impact of American Religious Liberalism*, notes: "Liberalism made that ["an intelligent modern and a serious Christian"] possible by providing the only way that he could be a Christian at all. It was not a choice, he says, of liberalism or the traditional faith. It was a choice between liberalism and no faith at all. He could not honestly believe

Strengths and Weaknesses of Fosdick's Life-Situation Preaching

Fosdick, had to be harmonized with the established truths and intellectual progress of modern culture. This being the case, one is hard pressed to find any kind of spirituality or doctrine of pneumatology in Fosdick's writing or theory of preaching.

A close reading of Fosdick's *As I See Religion* reveals that he believed that spiritual power was inwardly released. Much influenced by William James, he believed that the resource of spiritual power comes up through the subconscious into consciousness to release power for daily living. Such a vital experience, he claims, is the very essence of religion.[30] Nothing in Fosdick's thought suggests a belief in the Holy Spirit. He did not believe in unscientific miracles, which may account for the absence of pneumatology in his writings and sermons, which is not to say that he did not believe in God's spiritual presence.

The doctrine of the Holy Spirit, pneumatology, is central to Christianity. The pneumatological dimension is inseparable from all communication from God, and preaching that is not accompanied by pneumatological empowerment is mere human speech.[31] The Holy Spirit is the very life of God that accompanies the word of God, permitting the response for which God calls. God remains active within creation through the Holy Spirit. Christian preachers are called and ordained by Jesus Christ to preach in his name. For some critics, life-situation preaching fails to relate the Holy Spirit to Christian preaching. "In failing to relate preaching to the witness of the word," one author notes, "Fosdick has not adequately related preaching to the work of the Holy Spirit as the dynamic presence of God in Jesus Christ who alone can open the Word, open the minds and hearts of the congregation, and make the sermon to be the very Word of God addressed to the contemporary congregation."[32] Without the Holy Spirit, the preacher's spiritual eyes are blind to God's biblical truths. Life-situation preaching for Fosdick required "clairvoyance on the preacher's part into the thinking" of the people.[33] This "clairvoyance" (insight) supplants the role of the

---

in an inerrant Bible, the virgin birth, the traditional views of miracle, substitutionary atonement, Jesus as the second hypostasis of the Trinity, a fiery hell, the second coming of Jesus from the clouds, and all the other staple beliefs of traditional orthodoxy" (67).

30. Fosdick, *Religion*, 25.

31. Whatever else we call it, it is all human speech. It is human speech influenced by the Holy Spirit, or it is human speech that is not influenced by the Holy Spirit. But both are human speech.

32. Beverly, *Fosdick's Predigtweise*, 73.

33. Fosdick, *Autobiography*, 97.

Life-Situation Preaching for African-Americans

Holy Spirit in Fosdick's theory of preaching. The Holy Spirit works in and through the preacher to meet the spiritual needs of people.

James Alexander Forbes Jr., senior minister emeritus of the Riverside Church in New York City, served as pastor for 18 years, 1989–2007. Forbes was the fifth senior minister of the Riverside Church and the first African-American to serve in this capacity. Steeped in the Pentecostal tradition, Forbes reminds us that Jesus came preaching in the power of the Spirit, which is still a requirement for contemporary preaching. Forbes believes that effective preaching requires the presence and power of the Holy Spirit. He writes: "I do not know a conscientious preacher anywhere who would claim to preach without at least some acknowledgement of the aid of the Spirit, even if the minister did not tend to speak of it in that way. There are many preachers who are waiting for and depending on the power from beyond themselves—and there are many who are aware that if that power is not present, the preaching will not be effective."[34]

Preaching from day-to-day and week-to-week requires the enabling presence of the Holy Spirit. "We need some sense of the Spirit accompanied by power sufficient to interrupt a decline in the sense of the reality of God," explains Forbes.[35] His reference to "a decline in the sense of the reality of God" speaks to modernists' repudiation of the Holy Spirit for scientific verification.[36] He contends that the Spirit is at work or should be at work in every aspect of the preaching event, from communication to reception of the word of God.

Fosdick criticized his contemporaries because their approaches to Scripture seemed to resemble lectures. A criticism of equal weight can be levied against Fosdick's life-situation preaching and its failure to acknowledge the role of the Holy Spirit in preaching. Devoid of the Holy Spirit, the Bible, and the tradition of the church, life-situation preaching is simply a practical exercise or motivational talk about people's problems. The Holy Spirit empowers the preacher to preach God's word. On this view, the efficacy of Christian preaching is contingent upon the Holy Spirit's participation in the saving work of Jesus Christ and the work of the Holy Spirit in the believing heart. Through the power of the Holy Spirit, Christian preaching effects conviction, repentance, and salvation. Sermon composition is doable when the Holy Spirit is at work to guide the process: "The Spirit works

---

34. Forbes, Jr., *Holy Spirit and Preaching*, 21.
35. Ibid., 25.
36. Ibid.

Strengths and Weaknesses of Fosdick's Life-Situation Preaching

in sermon preparation and delivery to discern the heart and the situation of those who hear preaching and to guide their spiritual walk. This includes not only bringing persons to faith but also nurturing and deepening faith, which itself is a gift of the Spirit imparted through preaching."[37] Thus, Christian preaching relies on the empowerment of the Holy Spirit in every aspect of sermon preparation and delivery, and in every aspect of Christian ministry and living. Hence, any theory of preaching that does not consider or take seriously the work of the Holy Spirit is indeed an inchoate, if not ineffective, theory.

The problem, of course, is that it is difficult to determine with absolute certainty if a sermon is or is not the product of divinely inspired truths. At best, one hopes to feel the presence of God hovering over and permeating in the ecclesial community during the preaching event. Even in such a case, the preacher could be inspired by the Holy Spirit and the church may not be. One thing is for certain, though. Whenever the Holy Spirit is present, something happens, something transformative takes place. However favorable or unfavorable the sermon, something happens in the lives of listeners. In the face of such criticism regarding the Holy Spirit, it should be noted that, although Fosdick did not discuss the Holy Spirit as such, he did believe "that just as around our bodies is a physical universe from which we draw all our physical energy, so around our spirits is a spiritual Presence in living communion with whom we can find sustaining strength."[38] Fosdick believed wholeheartedly in God's spiritual presence.

The third criticism of Fosdick's life-situation preaching is that it is disconnected from the doctrine of the church. The church has a history and theology to which it belongs and which belongs to it. Fosdick revealed in his autobiography that both his friends and foes had difficulty defining his theological position. He believed that no "existent theology can be a final formulation of spiritual truth."[39] Accused of taking theology lightly, Fosdick responded: "I take theology so seriously that whenever in the Christian tradition I see doctrine persistently struggling over some central issue, displaced by new doctrine but still tussling with the same old problem, I am sure that the truth is really there, and that the combined transiency and persistence of doctrine in dealing with it is a testimony to its importance. So ideas of God change and ought to, but that fact does not mean that

---

37. Willimon and Lischer, s.v. "Holy Spirit and Preaching."
38. Fosdick, *Autobiography*, 75.
39. Ibid., 230.

Life-Situation Preaching for African-Americans

anything has happened to God."[40] Fosdick believed that theologies were psychologically and sociologically conditioned, and that dogmatism in theology is ridiculous. No scholar, if truth be told, has the whole truth about God, as human beings are finite and limited in intellectual capacity. For Fosdick, the individual was more important than the theology to which she subscribed. As such, theology changes or ought to change as humanity evolves. As he saw it, ministry was most useful to those persons who were religiously ruined by dogmatism, taught to identify the Christian gospel with some form of orthodoxy, as was true in his case. Their Christian experience, as was his, was at war with their intelligence. The problem for Fosdick was how to reconcile the Christian faith with modernity. To remedy this quandary, he disrobed himself of orthodox garb, thus severing his ties to the theology and doctrine of the church. The role of theology for Fosdick was to formulate, clarify, and interpret religious experience, not to provide fixed religious prescriptions.

In *The Modern Use of the Bible*, Fosdick, in typical liberal fashion, explicates the way in which theology should operate in interpreting experience. The critical approach to biblical theology, says Fosdick, does not try to harmonize the Bible with itself or apologize for the more immature portions of the Bible. Most important, Fosdick notes, the Bible restores the whole book in its unity as a progressive revelation of God. Fosdick wrestled with how the Bible could be useful to modern humanity. The phrase "abiding experiences and changing categories" speaks to his conclusion. By this he meant: "There are certain basic human experiences which are ever the same, but the mental framework in which these experiences are expressed changes from one time and place to another."[41] So understood, the task of the theologian is "to search out the abiding experiences which lie underneath the categories of the Bible and then to reinterpret and restate the meaning of these experiences in modern terms."[42]

---

40. Ibid., 231.

41. Fosdick, *Bible*, 129.

42. Ibid. In "The Significance of Dr. Fosdick in American Religious Thought," Reinhold Niebuhr, Fosdick's colleague at Union, stated that Fosdick's *Modern Use of the Bible* "embodies Fosdick's conviction that it is not necessary to exempt the historical elements of the Bible from a scrupulous historical scholarship to guard the faith" (4). Niebuhr believed that this book brought about "emancipation from biblicism and biblically-based obscurantism" and that Fosdick "understood how to make the biblical message relevant to the whole range of human problems" (ibid). This speaks tellingly to Fosdick's use of the Bible in preaching.

Strengths and Weaknesses of Fosdick's Life-Situation Preaching

Despite Fosdick's views about theology and dogma, the doctrine of the church is critically important for the life of the church. It helps the church to establish and defend its beliefs for all generations, as was the case of the Protestant Reformation of the sixteenth century. The Protestant Reformation led to the development of theological positions and literature (catechisms, confessions of faith, and works in systematic theology) to defend its ideas. The reformers were convinced that the Catholic Church had lost sight of its doctrine. Generally, protestant theologians recognize three levels of authority: Scripture, the creeds of Christendom, and the confessions of faith. The sixteenth century marked a period of critical reflection on the nature and identity of the church. Reformers such as Martin Luther and John Calvin argued for the need to return to Scripture—"by scripture alone" (*sola scriptura*)—as the primary and critical source of Christian theology.[43] This new emphasis upon Scripture had important implications for the church such as the rejection of beliefs not grounded in Scripture, and a new emphasis upon the public status of Scripture within the church.

Martin Luther proclaimed the doctrine of justification by faith alone (*sola fide*). It was Luther, a first-generation reformer, who made important contributions to the doctrine of grace—the center of the Christian gospel. It was John Calvin, a second-generation reformer, who made important contributions to the development of Protestant understandings of the church. For Calvin, the marks of a true church were that the word of God is preached and that the sacraments are rightly administered. This statement by Calvin represents the first attempt at a coherent and systematic Protestant ecclesiology. According to Calvin, the church is an institution that God uses to sanctify human beings and to work out the salvation of the elect. The point here is that the church has a long history of trying to understand its identity and purpose in light of contemporary life.

It is important to understand the history of the church in order to get a better sense of the church's purpose for our present day. As Beverly has well stated: "A Church that has forgotten its purpose and its message may desire to help people solve their problems, but it has lost its ability. A Church that looks at man in his contemporary dilemma before it looks at God and His Grace and Victory over the world has insight into neither the Word nor the World."[44] To be fair, Fosdick's goal was to be both "an intelligent modern and a serious Christian" and to make a contribution to the spiritual life of

---

43. McGrath, *Christian Theology*, 58.
44. Beverly, *Fosdick's Predigtweise*, 83.

his generation.[45] He wanted a credible faith with which to help people. This is respectable. The problem, however, is that his approach and writings do not reveal an organ link to the doctrine and theology of the church. For Fosdick, it was either Christian liberalism or no faith at all, as was stated previously in our discussion of his organic ingredients. He concluded that liberalism allowed him to have a credible faith, notwithstanding that he did not subscribe to staple beliefs of traditional orthodoxy.

Preaching is essential to the identity of the church. For life-situation critics, preaching that caters to people's need as the starting point of the sermon is lacking something vital. "But to begin with a problem and attempt to help people solve it through constructive faith and mystical experience is to base preaching on the preacher's insight into society and human nature," argues Beverly.[46] Fosdick's critics argue that his preaching was derived from the problems of his day without any discernable connection to the doctrine of the church. Their logic is typically arranged in this fashion: It was prudent of Fosdick to use the available knowledge of his day to meet people's needs; it was imprudent, however, to sever all ties with the source and historical significance of preaching, doctrine, and theology for the life and development of his congregation. Again, Beverly's counsel is helpful: "Any concept of preaching which leads to a lessening of the importance of preaching in the Church is not only an inadequate concept but it is a dangerous concept; for the preaching of the Word is one of the marks of the true Church and to eliminate it is to ultimately eliminate the existence of the Church itself."[47] Thus preaching is an integral part of the life of the Christian church, and preaching that does not take seriously the doctrine and theology of the church is lacking its historical roots in Christianity.

Fosdick's thoughts on and understanding of the church are scattered throughout his writings rather than a single systematic text. What one detects, however, is that he believed in an individualistic and voluntaristic institution grounded in Christian experience and oriented largely toward ethical concerns, rather than in dogma or tradition.[48] What this means is that the "sacramental, ritualistic, institutional, and doctrinal aspects of church life are necessarily subordinated to ethical matters."[49] Fosdick's

45. Fosdick, *Autobiography*, 55–57.
46. Beverly, *Fosdick's Predigtweise*, 83.
47. Ibid., 84.
48. Fosdick, "Personality-Centered Christianity," 82.
49. Fosdick, *Religion*, 22.

Strengths and Weaknesses of Fosdick's Life-Situation Preaching

view of the church is one of inclusivity, where the basis for membership is Christian experience. In *Christianity and Progress* he describes his idea of an inclusive church as a church that is the organizing center for all the Christian life of a community (as was the case at the Riverside Church). He expounded further that his idea of an inclusive church is not based upon theological conformity but upon the devotion to the Lord Jesus.

An inclusive church as Fosdick envisioned it is a church that harnesses the untapped goodwill and moral power of American communities. Fosdick believed that all Christians should work together for the good of humanity. His idea of an inclusive church is best understood as a church that desires to "be the point of incandescence where, regardless of denominationalism or theology, the Christian life of the community bursts into flame."[50] Fosdick stretches his idea of an inclusive church even further, saying: "The achievement of a worthy idea of God involves, therefore, the ability to discover God in all life, outside the Church as well as within, and in people who do not believe in him nor recognize him as well as in those who do."[51] He explains that God is too magnanimous to minister to people only after they have "confessedly receive[d] him."[52] Although Fosdick held unconventional views about the purpose and doctrine of the church, he nevertheless recognized the church's importance, as is evident when he writes:

> Many today think that they are getting on very well without the church, but have they ever pictured realistically what getting on without the church would mean? Let the church die, let generation after generation rise that never knew it, let Jesus become a myth, the Bible's message forgotten, faith in God vague and nebulous, worship finished, no more sacred music—only secular, no more religious education of the children—only secular, a literature from which have been deleted the ideas and ideals that have their

---

50. Fosdick, *Christianity and Progress*, 138. This book is a compilation of lectures that Fosdick delivered in 1922 for the Cole Lectureship at Vanderbilt University, School of Religion. The object of the lectureship was to present lectures in support of Christian religion. Here one finds a more extensive analysis of Fosdick's view of Christianity. The motivation for *Christianity and Progress* can be traced to a statement made by George William Knox, Professor of the Philosophy and History of Religion at Union Theological Seminary, to his class. Fosdick told Henry Sloan Coffin that Knox once said: "Be very careful how you baptize the modern belief in progress into the Christian faith." This for Fosdick was an eye-opener. See Coffin, *Union Theological Seminary*, 45.

51. Fosdick, *Christianity and Progress*, 139.

52. Ibid., 141.

Life-Situation Preaching for African-Americans

> rootage in the Christian, and all the leaven gone which the prophets implanted in our race—then we could live without the church. Who wants to try?[53]

The thought of a churchless society is not worth thoughtful consideration for Fosdick. Nevertheless, the church is rooted in a doctrinal history and theology that must be interpreted anew for each generation, not heedlessly overlooked or discarded.

Richard Lischer considered the question of the importance of theology for church in *A Theology of Preaching*. His conclusion was that much of what passes for theology does not draw its life from the gospel and is therefore utterly incapable of transforming lives or teaching and leading the church. He goes on to say that "only the preacher who is rooted (not buried) in the church's constitutive principles, its doctrine, will be free to address the concerns of living people."[54] Then, he says, because preaching "is rooted in those truths that touch humankind at its deepest levels—creation, identity, love, fulfillment, sin, hope, peace, forgiveness—becomes relevant without losing its soul." For Lischer, the first step toward regaining the ever-elusive relevance of preaching is accepting the doctrines of the church for their truth-value rather than their use-value. The preacher's theological faculty enables him to relate the human situation to the gospel, which makes the question of sermon-mechanics (where to start a sermon) less important:

> Where shall the preacher begin? With the contemporary, here-and-now? Or the biblical, then-and-there? When the preaching begins with the contemporary situation, it views that situation through the lens of the eternal gospel.[55] When the preaching begins with the biblical situation, it never offers it as exegetical "background," as though, in Fosdick's famous quip, people really come to church with a burning interest in the Jebusites, but rather it always associates the biblical situation with contemporary needs.[56]

Whether the preacher starts with the contemporary situation or the biblical situation, the infinite relevance of the gospel bridges the distance between these two worlds. Whatever the case, preaching is the first and final expression of theology, for the Christian movement was born in preaching.

53. Fosdick, *Faith for Tough Times*, 77.
54. Lischer, *Theology of Preaching*, 16.
55. Ibid., 21–22.
56. Ibid., 21.

Strengths and Weaknesses of Fosdick's Life-Situation Preaching

Fosdick's life-situation preaching did not have the parameters of theology and doctrine to help contain it, to keep it in line with the church. Consequently, his preaching was, at times, theologically light, and, at other times, theologically vacuous. When preaching becomes weak and watered-down, theology and doctrine are there to revivify it. When preaching loses sight of the gospel, theology and doctrine are there to shine new light on the mystery of the gospel. Hence it is imperative for the preacher to understand and accept the doctrine and theology of the church as a schoolmaster to help guide the preacher in relating the eternal gospel to the contemporary "mind and milieu of the listener."[57]

A notable weakness of Fosdick's life-situation preaching is that it does not take into consideration the life situations of nonwhite listeners, specifically African-Americans. Whereas Fosdick maintained that the aim of the sermon is to help people solve their real problems, the African-American sermon aims to present scriptural evidence of God's sovereignty, justice, and presence amid oppression, marginalization, and injustice. The African-American homiletic is unique because it originated in and is shaped by the unique sociocultural experience of African-Americans. Fosdick's life-situation preaching, on the other hand, was centered in the "life situations"—values, interests, problems, and experiences—of upper middle-class and upper class liberal, white listeners. As noted previously, Fosdick maintained that the only justifiable aim of a sermon was to help people solve their problems. Needless to say, his intended audience was not society's oppressed and marginalized. A close reading of his sermons and published texts confirm as much. Nor did his definition of "problems" take into consideration the unique problems of African-Americans. The fact is, Fosdick's life-situation preaching reflected the life situations of white listeners, who had markedly different life situations from African-Americans.

In short, although Fosdick's homiletic has its distinctive qualities, it represents the white homiletic tradition. The African-American homiletic, with its elements of life-situation preaching, originated in and speaks to the unique sociocultural context of African-Americans. This is the point of departure for African-American preaching. It is rooted in and true to the black experience in America and throughout diaspora. Every preacher seeks to understand and interpret Scripture in light of both the preacher's and the listeners' sociocultural experience. This is the norm. To be sure, no homiletic—white, black, or other—is without subjectivity, implied

---

57. Ibid., 20.

assumptions, or theories regarding sermon composition, delivery, and expectation. The variety and diversity of African-American preaching theories and styles notwithstanding, the African-American preacher's goal is to convince and remind African-American listeners that there is a sovereign God who acts mightily on behalf of the marginalized, oppressed, disinherited, and powerless people in our society and world.

The unique experience of African-Americans is the starting place for the African-American sermon. From beginning to end, the sermon presents indisputable scriptural evidence of God's historical and contemporary presence with the oppressed in their struggle for liberation from oppressive sociocultural realities. The African-American preacher is experientially and viscerally attuned to the unique aspects of the African-American experience, and thus is qualified to speak to oppressed people on behalf of God. Whereas Fosdick's life-situation preaching most assuredly emphasized people's problems, the African-American homiletic emphasizes survival, first, and matters of life, second, all while conveying that God is unmistakably present to bring about both personal and societal transformation. No message is more critical and urgent than this in the African-American preaching event.

African-Americans have had to deal with the repudiation of their humanity, the disaffirmation of their blackness, and the deprivation of basic civil and human rights. In light of this, heightened attention is called to what the Christian gospel says to the "least of these." Given the profundity of African-Americans' sociocultural context, Fosdick's mere problem-solution formulaic is, to some extent, inadequate. In a very real sense, the African-American preacher knows that the oppressive conditions and unique experiences of African-Americans have their origin and staying power in cultural, social, political, and economic forces that suffocate and destroy black life. Unlike many of the problems that Fosdick addressed in his preaching, these forces warrant a different approach to preaching, for there is no easy solution or quick fix to these enduring, debilitating problems.

The African-American sermon, therefore, must imbue its listeners with hope that a God of sufficient and matchless power is acting in concrete and practical ways to transform their lives. In the final analysis, Fosdick's understanding and interpretation of life situations, and thus the benefits of life-situation preaching, is colored and limited by his own parochial understanding of nonwhite people, by his sociocultural and socioeconomic status, and by his experiences as an educated, white liberal preacher in

Strengths and Weaknesses of Fosdick's Life-Situation Preaching

America. It is true, nevertheless, that Fosdick's life-situation preaching has enduring homiletic value for contemporary preachers. In the chapter that follows, I will explore Fosdick's message to young people regarding Christian ministry.

5

The Christian Vocation and Life-Situation Preaching

Christian Vocation

Fosdick had an enduring concern for young people. He preached in chapels around the nation, leaving an indelible imprint on young minds. College students were attracted to his ministry. He talked frequently at conferences and retreats for college students. He had a vested interest in young men and women because the future of the church was theirs.[1] In *The Atlantic Monthly* Fosdick candidly addressed young men and women considering and entering Christian ministry. In his introductory remarks, he discussed the need for Protestant churches to expand their thinking regarding diversified opportunities in ministry.[2]

Highlighting the contrast between Roman Catholicism and Protestantism, Fosdick believed that the latter can learn from the former. He observed that Roman Catholicism developed and trained young ministers according to their special gifts and then placed them in various types of roles, from administrators to preachers to scholars. On the other hand, he saw the Protestant ministry as being more narrowly defined, offering only two forms of service: pastoral ministry and preaching. In particular, notes

1. Macnab, "Fosdick at First Church," 33.
2. Fosdick, "The Christian Ministry," 63.

The Christian Vocation and Life-Situation Preaching

Fosdick, the Protestant minister had been expected to preach, which is the center of the worship service. The call to be a Protestant clergyman had always been a call to preach, he observed. He noticed a paradigmatic shift afoot in Protestant circles; young men and women were beginning to specialize in a particular area of ministry. Despite the expectation for ministers to be multifunctional experts (janitor, fundraiser, religious educator, civic leader, administrator), Protestant churches were selecting young men and women for specialized service in the church according to their abilities.

Fosdick saw how centralized populations equated to fewer but larger churches, with more diversified functions and with staffs of clergy representing abilities to perform these roles. The momentum for this phenomenon was transportation and rapid communication—automobiles, public transportation, and the radio—that forced small local congregations to combine into more centralized churches with expanded ministries. Fosdick cited church statistics by an expert who estimated that in a year there was an increase in church members of 573,723 and a decrease in the number of churches of 1470. The centralization of ministry meant increasingly varied ministry opportunities for young men and women. As a result, men and women with no experience in preaching still had a place in Christian ministry, although they had a different specialty. This, for Fosdick, was a hopeful sign.

As Fosdick saw it, Protestant churches were unprepared to absorb and use the abilities of these young men and women. Nevertheless, the situation, as Fosdick tells it, was hopeful for young men and women preparing for ministry:

> Many youths who feel neither the ability nor the wish to preach are going, as they supremely desire to go, into the service of their generation's spiritual life. They will be ministers of religion and servants of the church. The result will be a far richer and more varied leadership for the forces of organized faith and a far more satisfying career for many young men and women who, not commercially minded, desire above all else to make a contribution to religion.[3]

The point here is that diversified opportunities are attractive to young people who are considering ministry but are reluctant because they have to preach when they do not want to. Others, who do want to preach will be

---

3. Ibid., 60.

saved from "an immeasurable quantity of midweek religious talk."[4] This is not to say that the role of the preacher will change. Rather, preachers will be selected for ministry in their area of interest. According to Fosdick, Protestantism emphasized and relied too much on preaching to the unintended neglect of other ministry opportunities and functions. What the Protestant church needed, in his estimate, was young men and women who were motivated to change and not serve the "ecclesiastical status quo." To this point he said: "No one has any business to go into the ministry who is satisfied with the churches as they are. We have too many complacent ministers now."[5] This, for Fosdick, was a clarion call for young ministerial prospects to exercise leadership in Protestant churches, even if such leadership meant going against the grain of traditional Protestant leadership.

Fosdick's Advice to Young Aspirants to Ministry

To the young minister considering the preaching ministry, Fosdick advises that such one "aim first at recovering the accent of reality in the pulpit."[6] Long gone is the day when the preacher was the leading expert in education and information, Fosdick explains. The preacher no longer holds this dominant position. The preacher's dilemma is that people in the pews are just as educated and have as much, if not more, knowledge and education. This, according to Fosdick, is a godsend, for it "forces the wise preacher to quit his reliance on ecclesiastical authority, to cut out cant, bombast, hokum, or whatever represents the cheap substitution of wordiness for genuineness, and to make of his sermons a forthright endeavor to deal in a real way with the real problems of real people."[7] In essence, the dominant place of the minister in education and information is no longer a reality and, as a result, young men and women preparing for the preaching ministry should endeavor to compose sermons that address the way in which people think about their personal and spiritual problems. No preacher can be an expert in every field; therefore, the preacher does well to be skilled in the tools of the homiletical trade. The young preacher's main business in the pulpit is to compose thought-provoking, life-transforming sermons that speak intelligibly to life situations.

4. Ibid., 61.
5. Ibid.
6. Ibid.
7. Ibid., 62.

The Christian Vocation and Life-Situation Preaching

Not only should the young minister strive to preach well, but also to serve as a director of public worship. Protestant churches have overemphasized preaching and deemphasized public worship, in Fosdick's view. Roman Catholics go to church to worship, and the center of worship is the sacrament. The sacrament symbolizes inclusiveness, as all sorts of people participate in worship together. Worship is inclusive, whereas a sermon is selective; "it appeals to a certain mental stratum; it automatically excludes from its range of interest other types of mind than the kind from which it comes."[8] This accounts for, in Fosdick's thinking, the class organization of churches. All this is not to say that preaching should be diminished in worship, but rather that the beauty of worship should be taken seriously alongside the sermon. Fosdick attributes the decline of interest in and concern for public worship to the way in which it has been conducted. Public worship does business in human souls, notes Fosdick. What is this business? "It causes people who have been looking down to look up. It reorients life, redirects energy, freshens ideals, restores equilibrium, and liberates spiritual resources."[9]

In addition to preaching well and serving well as a director of public worship, the young preacher should take advantage of the opportunity for intellectual leadership. The distaste of university ministries, students' abstention from religious practices, the agnosticism on campuses, and the contemporary waywardness of the day all constitute an opportunity for the preacher. "If he is alive to the situation," Fosdick remarks, "he will quit his reliance on creedal authority, and instead of standing outside the turmoil and confusion of this generation's endeavor to find an intelligible religion, he will get inside it."[10] Such problems are but an opportunity for the intelligent and adventurous preacher to exhibit leadership by presenting the way to a more credible faith. According to Fosdick, the problem is not one of irreligiosity: "This generation is not irreligious; it is intensely concerned with religion; but it will not, in its intelligent areas, be content with creedal conventionality. It cannot patiently harbor a modern worldview on one side and on the other a formulation of religions which contradicts it."[11] In sum, Fosdick believed that the urgent need of the church is first-rate

---

8. Ibid., 63.
9. Ibid., 64.
10. Ibid., 65.
11. Ibid.

Life-Situation Preaching for African-Americans

intellectual leadership to help clarify and reconstruct the thinking of Protestant churches.

The final word on this matter is that young women and men entering ministry should have a clear intent to help harness the spiritual power of the church to help solve our social problems. The church is an enormous resource of spiritual power. Preachers can be instrumental in helping church members think through the major problems of our economic and international life, for the church has been slow to recognize and understand the relationship of these problems and their religious convictions. Fosdick holds that the preacher is the most qualified person to help church members understand the application of Christian ethics to the problems of our day. If ignorance and bigotry imperil the church, then how can American society remain untouched? The church has the capacity to be either a bastion for or barrier to social justice and societal transformation. The importance of the preacher's cognizance regarding resources of spiritual power is to instruct the church therein and to save American society from irreparable loss.

In "To Those Interested in the Profession of the Ministry," Fosdick argued that the Christian ministry cannot reasonably appeal to soft minds desiring a conventional profession. He surmised the collapse of traditional ecclesiastical organization. Such a collapse, he maintains, "is going to be uncomfortable to formal and stereotyped clergymen."[12] As regards the collapse among mainline Protestant churches, Fosdick spoke prophetically: "Personally, I think that there is bound to be a great mortality among sectarian churches in the next twenty-five to fifty years. The old type of church, centered denominationally in the peculiarities of some sect, has outlived its usefulness and cannot minister to the deepest needs of the American people. As the old type of church dies out, however, a new type comes in."[13] Fosdick underestimated denominationalism and overestimated nondenominationalism. He was correct, however, in his forecast concerning the burgeoning of nondenominational churches. For Fosdick, the religious problem in America boils down to intellectual and religious leadership. A leader, in his assessment, is a person with intelligence, character, and insight into the religious problems of our day. Taking a reflective page from his own ministry, especially during the fundamentalist-modernist controversy, Fosdick explains that Christian ministry needs leaders who are not afraid of conflict. "He who continually shrinks from conflict," writes John

---

12. Fosdick, "Profession of Ministry," 69.
13. Ibid., 71.

The Christian Vocation and Life-Situation Preaching

A. Broadus, "should stir himself up to faithfulness; he who is by nature belligerent should cultivate forbearance and courtesy."[14]

To young women and men considering the Christian ministry for salary, respectability, and professional routine or occupation, Fosdick sternly advises, "Stay out."[15] In response to a highly secularized, materialistic society, he says that the challenge of Christian ministry, which is also its opportunity, is to help society recover the abiding spiritual values of life. Such an undertaking is reserved for the intelligent Christian leader who understands the religious problem in America and is prepared to address the problem with a mind untrammeled by conventional wisdom and unrestricted of sectarian shackles. Notwithstanding Fosdick's critique of Protestant churches, he insists that "the living gospel is too much alive for any church's failures utterly to deaden it."[16] When at their best, churches are institutions where "lives are transformed, character is built, courage is renewed, faith is strengthened, ideals of personal and social conduct which otherwise would die are kept alive, public-spirited devotion is engendered, and God's kingdom of righteousness on earth is made a living hope."[17]

In the final analysis, Fosdick believed that young men and women considering Christian ministry face unique challenges, awesome opportunities, and endless possibilities. This holds true for contemporary ministry as well. There are unprecedented challenges facing the church. In the face of such challenges, the church is in dire need of young, intelligent, and courageous leaders who can bring its collective spiritual resources, intellectual power, and physical energy to bear on the multifarious, multifaceted problems of our day. This calls for young women and men of vision who can help the church better understand and respond to the religious, social, economic, and political forces that impact the church, society, culture, community, and the world. The Christian pulpit is and has been one of the most powerful forces of change in American social, religious, and cultural life. The transformation of the world is but one event away, and the church, with God as its navigator and courageous leadership at its helm, can lead the transformation.

---

14. Broadus, *Preparation and Delivery of Sermons*, 65.
15. Fosdick, "Profession of Ministry," 70.
16. Fosdick, *Faith for Tough Times*, 77–78.
17. Ibid.

Life-Situation Preaching for African-Americans

Contemporary Life-Situation Preaching

Fosdick witnessed the decline of white mainline churches in America and the increase of nondenominational, nonsectarian churches. To discuss whether Fosdick was right or wrong is beyond the scope of this book. This crisis, as he saw it, called for intellectual Christian leadership. Prominent in his writings and speeches is an invitation to young preachers to exercise Christian leadership. He believed that the young preachers of his day could make a spiritual contribution to the church and society. Fosdick's advice to the clergy of his day stemmed from his knowledge and personal experiences. His preeminent concern was to relate the gospel to the concrete needs of his people. In fact, nothing mattered more to Fosdick than to meet the urgent spiritual needs of those to whom he preached with the intellectual resources at his disposal. He once said in a lecture to clergy: "Generations differ in their most urgent needs. History could be written in terms of the varied intellectual and spiritual problems which, from age to age, have pressed up into the crucial focus of attention; and in our time, tottering with worldwide convulsions, this problem which we are considering the impermanent, the durable amid the fugitive, is now a matter of life and death."[18] Our contemporary context is much different from Fosdick's context. Still, some of the problems that vexed people then are the same problems that vex people today, even though the nature of the problems differs.

Although the context has changed dramatically, people's psychological, physical, spiritual, social, and emotional needs remain the same. As one author pointed out, "It's not so much that needs have changed but how people perceived them."[19] In light of this, life-situation preaching has a future in American Protestant churches even though old ways of doing ministry are no longer viable. Young preachers in white and black mainline churches today are going to have to wrestle with cultural shifts and their implications for ministry. Congregations today consist of younger Christians who are generally distrustful of authority in its various forms: ecclesiastical, biblical, theological, or hierarchical.[20] Therefore, it is important for preachers

---

18. Ibid., 14.

19. Johnston, *Preaching to a Postmodern World*, 71.

20. Kitchens, *Postmodern Parish*, 57. Kitchens has influenced my thinking regarding postmodern Christian leadership. Commenting on the differences between moderns and postmoderns, he observed: "They aren't necessarily pressing for us to drop our commitment to an educated clergy. They are not as willing as Christians before them

The Christian Vocation and Life-Situation Preaching

"to have an awareness of the ambiguities and uncertainties that are in the hearts of many Christians" in the pews.[21] As long as life-situation preaching continues to address the felt needs of listeners, there is going to be an audience for the life-situation preacher.

Fosdick's practical approach to preaching has implications for young men and women considering the ministry. This is not to say that the preacher has to start the sermon with a felt need in the same way that Fosdick did. No, not at all. It is to say, rather, that the practice that undergirded Fosdick's approach to preaching provides young preachers with a paradigm for sermon composition that helps them connect with their audience. People get bored when the sermon does not involve them, speak to them, or move them. In fact, people process information better when it directly affects their lives. Life-situation preaching seeks to effectively involve the listener in the communication process by creating an atmosphere where it seems as though the preacher is speaking directly to the individual—an atmosphere that is conducive to the receptivity of the proclamation of the gospel. So, in light of this, what are the implications of Fosdick's life-situation preaching for young preachers?

In the first place, preachers must understand the needs of their listeners. If the preacher is going to take advantage of life-situation preaching, she has to be able to speak directly to people's needs and attempt to solve their spiritual problems. This can be quite difficult. Acquiring insight into human nature takes time. Yet, it is the preacher's responsibility to grapple with the profound problems of the day and provide biblical insight to help facilitate healing and restoration. Consequently, young preachers do well to become students of human nature. They must study people empirically, for there is epistemological value in human experience that cannot be learned from inorganic material. Such an endeavor is best done through pastoral counseling. In the consultation room, confidential information is divulged that provides insight into human nature and reveals the deepest issues that beset human beings. People come to the minister in the hope that he can help them in some spiritual or practical way, or both.

Analyzing people's needs is one thing, brainstorming practical solutions is another. This process necessitates constant consultation with books,

---

were, however, to accept the pastor's authority unquestioningly or to accept the clergy's interpretation of scripture without an opportunity for other voices and points of view to be heard and considered by community" (57).

21. Allen, Blaisdell, and Johnston, *Theology for Preaching*, 29.

Life-Situation Preaching for African-Americans

advice from other more experienced ministers and professionals, and quiet reflection. To say to young preachers that they are to solve other people's problems induces a strong disinclination toward Christian ministry. Truly, that is a tall order for even the experienced pastor. Nevertheless, Fosdick's preaching ministry gives us hope and encouragement that it can be done well. Is it the minister's job to "solve the people's problems?" What about the ecclesia, the church, a communal group? It's not just the preacher but the *ekklesia* working together to solve the problems. The minister is not in it by herself. The entire church community is obligated to aid in such problem solving.

Fosdick had routines that helped him to become and stay an effective preacher. He read voraciously, and he advised young preachers to do the same, as his biographer observed: "He advised younger ministers always to have a book within reach to take advantage of every spare moment and also to make every vacation a reading spree."[22] It is said that Fosdick read multiple books simultaneously. He kept a book in his desk drawer in his office at church; one at his seminary office; always took one with him on the train; and kept one in his home office.[23] Fosdick was in constant search of resources to bring to bear on people's needs. That the preacher should read the Bible daily for spiritual sustenance goes without saying. That the young preacher should read the Bible for spiritual resources to meet the people's needs also goes without saying. What should be said, however, is that the preacher must read more than the Bible if he or she is to provide both spiritual and intellectual leadership for people.

Fosdick had an affinity for biography, but he also read biblical theology, history, economics, and psychology. He was fed intellectually on a diet of biography, as this genre gave him keen insight into people's lives—their high hopes and disillusionments, problems and solutions, handicaps and strengths, fears and courage, successes and failures. Many of Fosdick's sermon illustrations were derived from biography. It is safe to say, then, that perennial engagement with intellectual resources made Fosdick an organic intellectual and an effective preacher. Notwithstanding that Fosdick was more concerned with intellectual development than spiritual formation, he was masterful in his use of life-situation preaching. The young preacher determined to pursue a Christian vocation should seek to immerse oneself

---

22. Miller, *Fosdick*, 353.
23. Ibid.

The Christian Vocation and Life-Situation Preaching

not only in people's lives but also in books, historical and contemporary, for professional development.

In the second place, young preachers do well to understand that their lack of experience does not mean that they cannot make a meaningful spiritual contribution to contemporary ministry and society. Life-situation preaching gives hope to the young preacher and the novice preacher. Even talented preachers, confident in their abilities and sure of their calling, will find value in life-situation preaching as a means to address questions that people are asking, problems that people are facing, and experiences that are troubling them privately, socially, or professionally. Regardless of one's credentials (or the lack thereof), the life-situation preacher can bring about the transformation of personality through effective preaching and ministry. Diffidence dissipates; confidence emerges. Such preachers will connect with their listeners because they are showing an interest in the concrete problems that are the source of discord in people's lives. The young preacher's sermons will be relevant, timely, and will have a meaningful impact on the listeners.

It is true that young preachers determined to be Christian ministers are met with entrenched skepticism because of their immaturity and inexperience. It is also true that such skepticism is inextricably linked to preconceived notions about young people. Changing people's perception and challenging conventional wisdom is difficult but not impossible. The way in which young preachers conduct themselves in preaching (handling the Word), teaching (handling information), and counseling (handling people) can help the congregation to develop a clear picture of the preacher's maturity and potential. No young preacher need feel inadequate for ministry as long as the preacher is willing to invest in his or her spiritual and intellectual development. It has been said by preachers of old that God desires the human being's heart. While this is true, it is also true that God desires the mind. Both the mind and the heart have to be unlocked from the inside.

The young preacher, as was the case with Fosdick, must seek to be a serious Christian and *intellectual* leader. Fosdick came into his own after years of preaching. He suffered many disappointments and setbacks in life. As a neophyte preacher, he spent many a long day in frustration over sermon composition. It was not until he was utterly fed-up that he experimented with an approach to preaching that he found meaningful and indispensable. If nothing else, the young preacher does well to study various approaches to preaching and use the approach that is best suited

Life-Situation Preaching for African-Americans

for the preacher's ministry. Regardless of the approach, extreme care must be taken to ensure that the gospel of Jesus Christ is brought to bear on the concrete problems of the congregation. The life-situation approach only becomes a message to people's self-centeredness when the sermon both begins and ends with a human need, excluding the role of the Bible and Holy Spirit in the process. Be that as it may, no resource however enlightening, is as relevant and as potent and as transformative as the gospel of Jesus Christ.

In the third place, life-situation preaching helps young preachers to understand the relationship between pastoral counseling and preaching as means to provide life to, and insight for, the preacher's sermon. At the heart of ministry is the need for the preacher and ecclesial community to effectively deal with and handle the urgent needs of troubled personalities. This is what makes the pastoral calling different from other callings. Preaching that speaks from an in-depth understanding of beliefs, values, and assumptions gives the preacher instant credibility, for it offers the preacher the opportunity to connect with the hearts and minds of the congregation. Fosdick once said that he envied young ministers who were trained in pastoral psychology. He regretted not having had such training.

Young ministers today have a pastoral advantage because they have an opportunity to receive training that makes personal counseling effective. The application of psychology to the pastoral vocation provides an ideal situation where the pastor is able to provide professional counseling and the counselee is able to receive quality pastoral counseling, thereby addressing the counselee's urgent needs. "No minister," argues Fosdick, "who practices personal counseling can long remain in an ivory tower."[24] Personal counseling allows the preacher to share vicariously in the struggles of human beings with every kind of problem known to humanity. The point here, which bears repeating, is that personal counseling provides insight into people's lives and better equips the young preacher to address today's listener with clarity and relevance.

Young preachers must take it upon themselves to think deeply about the context in which they provide ministry and begin to experiment with approaches to preaching that consists of fidelity to the word of God, spiritual substance and intellectual food to listeners, and practical feasibility in sermon composition for the preacher. What is more, these preachers must seek to make the God of yesterday and yesteryear attractive to the technologically-oriented, social media-engrossed minds of today.

---

24. Fosdick, *Autobiography*, 219.

The Christian Vocation and Life-Situation Preaching

Notwithstanding that over six decades separate us from Fosdick's preaching ministry, his method of preaching has qualities that are important for and relevant to contemporary preaching. This is not to say that one should accept wholesale each aspect of Fosdick's approach to preaching, but that contemporary preaching can benefit from his practical approach to preaching. While it is true that the social situation for preaching has changed drastically, especially given the technological revolution, it is also true, as Fosdick pointed out, that people are still concerned with their problems and how to understand and interpret their problems in light of the Gospel. Human nature is still the same, to be sure. And the Gospel is as relevant today as it was in Fosdick's time.

Effective preaching harmonizes the problems of the people and the gospel in an imaginative way that helps to shed light on and provide answers to people's real problems. Fred Craddock said it best when he advised: "Some older volumes on preaching could profitably be reissued, not as a sentimental return to old paths but as a confession that part of the malaise in the discipline is due not to a stubborn refusal to move beyond tradition but to a thoughtless failure to listen carefully to that tradition."[25] To revisit Fosdick's method is not to repudiate contemporary, casual forms of preaching, but rather to reassess the effectiveness of his method in light of unimaginativeness in contemporary preaching.

This has certainly not been a comprehensive analysis of all the implications of life-situation preaching for the contemporary young preacher in a mainline church. However, it has been a discourse on some of the salient advantages of life-situation preaching. The emphasis in this chapter has been on young people. However, the information delineated here is universal in that any preacher can benefit from this approach to preaching, including those who preach and minister to African-American listeners, which is taken up in chapter 6, the final chapter in this book.

---

25. Craddock, *Preaching*, 14.

6

Preaching to African-Americans' Life Situations

African-American Life-Situation Preaching

Fosdick did not believe that one's racial or national background served as a proper test of membership in a Christian church. On the contrary, he believed that racial and national variety enriched Christian fellowship. The Riverside Church, with its interdenominational, nonsectarian character, was an interracial fellowship, although I suspect that not many blacks attended in relation to the number of whites.[1] Members were accepted on the basis of their Christian faith and not race, color, or nationality. Fosdick did not expand upon his convictions regarding African-Americans except to say that he abhorred racial discrimination and injustice. He hoped that his grandchildren would participate in the fight against racial prejudice and discrimination.

Yet he was removed, so it seems, from the perilous plight and egregious social conditions of African-Americans, for he said that the most critical and contentious social problem of his generation was WWI.[2] While

---

1. Fosdick, *Autobiography*, 199–200.

2. Ibid., 292. Rufus Burrow Jr., a close reader of the manuscript version of this book, noted that when one is not the immediate victim of a social problem like racism, such a one can identify some other social problem as "the most contentious" of one's generation. He points out that Martin Luther King Jr. and Bobby Kennedy were assassinated in 1968,

Preaching to African-Americans' Life Situations

it is true that WWI created intricate and pervasive social problems for America, it is also true the Armistice created intense discrimination and hostility for many African-American veterans. Indeed, it is intellectually indigestible the extent to which African-American soldiers, returning from war after risking their lives in combat, were accorded the insufferable indignities of being forbidden entry into restaurants at various military bases in the segregated south that opened their doors to German prisoners of war, or were humiliated and beaten by police officers for trying to feed themselves in a railroad station restaurant, not to mention the unspeakable horror of being maimed, castrated, or lynched.

As Fosdick's biographer noted, "Fosdick was a child of his time, but it is, nevertheless, necessary to make the hard observation that this crusader for racial justice never quite comprehended the depth and breadth of racism in America and never displayed the sensitive understanding of the black experience one might hope from an author of psychological studies."[3] He, like many whites of his generation, "was unable totally to transcend the cultural conditioning of the white racist society in which he lived."[4] To note these instances of racism is not to suggest that Fosdick was a racist by any stretch of the imagination. Nothing could be further from the truth. Although he was a man of his time, he did not subscribe to racial prejudice or discrimination. He categorically denounced racism; and judged racism and de facto segregation as unchristian.

Fundamentally, Fosdick believed that racism was the evilest thing in the world, and he concurred with Booker T. Washington that "we can be as separate as the five fingers, and yet as one as the hand."[5] Although he "never stared down the muzzle of a redneck's shotgun or felt the shock of a sheriff's cattle prod or the bite of an attack dog or shared a jail cell with lunch-counter demonstrators," he did appeal to Congress to pass antilynching legislation, sponsored rallies supporting such legislation, and sat on a number of committees and organizations (Interracial Fellowship of Greater New York, the Interracial Music Council, the Citizens' Committee in Harlem, to name a few) committed to the elimination of racial

and yet there are white Americans who remember the record of the USC football team as being the most important event that year. Fosdick, like so many white liberals of his day knew full well that racism was a sin, but their "whiteness" prevented them from seeing it as a more serious social evil than war.

3. Miller, *Fosdick*, 451–52.
4. Ibid., 455.
5. Ibid., 454.

discrimination.[6] In any event, Fosdick never communicated—perhaps never thought through—the implications and merits of his life-situation preaching for nonwhites.

The uniqueness of the black experience in America warrants an analysis of the benefits of life-situation preaching for African-Americans. The critical question is whether young Africa-American preachers and the black church can benefit from Fosdick's life-situation preaching. What, for example, does life-situation preaching say to the existential social problems that continue to plague the African-American community, such as intra-community and intraracial (black-on-black) violence, and police brutality? Such exclusive American social issues adversely affect the spiritual, mental, and psychological wellbeing of America's black masses. There is no doubt that Fosdick's life-situation preaching is relevant to the African-American church and community today. Fosdick tailored his preaching for the ears of white, middle-class Americans. He was, after all, a white, middle-class pastor who served predominantly upper- and middle-class white, sophisticated congregations. Needless to say, Fosdick's white audiences benefited from his preaching ministry and so can the African-American listeners. Better yet, young African-American preachers can apply the best that life-situation preaching has to offer to the existential life situations of their community. How do young, motivated African-American preachers get at this vital task?

The conscientious African-American preacher must be able to speak directly and intelligently to the unique needs and "life situations" of African-Americans. Preaching that takes seriously the life situations of African-American listeners starts with the existential situations that affect the quality of life for those "who stand with their backs against the wall," to use the apt phrase of Howard Thurman.[7] Arguably, the efficacy of any sermon, especially the life-situation sermon, is the extent to which it brings the timely and timeless truths of the Bible to bear on the social, economic, political, and cultural forces that affect listeners. The truth is, the disinherited masses can little care about homiletical correctness, whether the sermon begins with the Bible or the life situation of listeners, as long as the sermon speaks emphatically to their unique lived experiences and existential realities with the gospel. Preaching to socially ostracized, economically deprived, politically powerless, educationally deprived people—the lower

---

6. Ibid., 457.
7. Thurman, *Jesus and the Disinherited*, 1.

class and underclass of society—is radically different from preaching to people in other hierarchical social categories such as upper and middle classes.

There is something to be said, though, for preaching that starts therapeutically where African-American listeners ache the most. If the preacher starts with listeners' acute pain, then the preacher will have their undivided attention, as the preacher will be dealing with issues of critical importance to their short- and long-term survival. For African-American listeners, such preaching is exhilarating because it addresses their urgent needs and personal and social problems with the power and proclamation of the gospel in relatable terms. In what follows, I will discuss two of the most foremost and formidable problems affecting the black community: black-on-black violence, and police brutality. I will give more sustained attention to the former than the latter, and then briefly discuss how life-situation preaching can help address these problems.[8]

Black-on-Black Violence

One of the most critical problems affecting the African-American community is the epidemic of black-on-black violence that is ravaging the lives of young black males in America's inner cities. The phenomenon of self-destructive behavior and the atrophy of values is nowhere more prevalent than in America's smothering ghettoes. The general factors associated with black-on-black violence are low socioeconomic background, single parent households, economically-deprived urban and central-city areas, and higher rates of death in black populations where many are unemployed or have low incomes.[9] This is true for both the victim and the offender. Many of the victims and offenders come from socially and economically oppressed homes. They have difficulty identifying with the larger society. Social disintegration, economic and educational deprivation, unemployment and underemployment all contribute to the dismal social phenomena that exist in far too many of America's African-American communities.

James P. Comer says that traumatized black families—socially and economically disempowered—deteriorated most in the face of a changing

---

8. I do not address some of the debilitating issues (indolence, irresponsibleness, a sense of entitlement, etc.) that exists among some African-Americans.

9. Palley and Robinson, "Black on Black Crime," 59–62.

economy.[10] Of such families, he notes that they are the primary site of a disproportionate amount of violence and other social problems. It should be noted here that there are fundamental systemic and structural forces—e.g., racism, economic exploitation, racial profiling, discrimination, injustice, and so forth—that contribute to the social issues in African-American communities. Thus, the reasons for these issues are more extensive and intricate than merely the lack personal ethics, moral character, and selflove. As is true with all communities, there are systemic and structural forces that African-Americans have no control over.

The conscientious young African-American preacher must understand the general factors associated with black-on-black violence and the intricate dynamics of black existence in America. A life-situation sermon should not only address these factors but it should also discuss how to prevent them and how to live more faithfully as Christians in the face of them. God is the divine architect who designed the foundation upon which all preaching rests, and the architectural structure of the black sermon consists of the existential life situations of African-American listeners.

James W. Clarke has observed that since 1964 approximately half of the violent crime committed each year in the United States is attributable to young black males, who represent less than 3 percent of the total population.[11] Clarke traces the origins and nature of black-on-black violence to the southern experience and the system of criminal justice that took the place of slavery as a means of social control after emancipation. He notes that whites cared little about who was murdered, raped, or robbed as long as such crimes did not affect white interests. When blacks victimized whites, allegedly or factually, the consequences involved lynching, burning, bludgeoning, discriminatory capital sentencing, and convict labor. Southern prosecutors and defense attorneys did not take black-on-black crime seriously. "Thus the term 'Negro law' emerged after emancipation to describe such judicial indifference and the existence of a different standard of justice," explains Clarke.[12]

The extent to which a crime was punishable under law was determined by its effect on the white community. The result was that black crimes went unchecked by law enforcement and, as a result, a form of personal law enforcement was established. Clarke notices three enduring consequences of

10. Ibid., 60. Palley and Robinson cite James P. Comer.
11. Clarke, "Black-on-Black Violence," 46.
12. Ibid., 47.

personal law enforcement. First, leniency and often immunity for crimes committed against blacks; second, it encouraged black-on-black violence; third, it contributed directly to the disruption, disunity, and increased rates of violent crimes within the black community and black family.[13] Another factor that Clarke discusses is the ease with which blacks could obtain handguns. In the early twentieth century, handguns in hardware stores and pawn shops were readily available for a few dollars. Handguns provided black males with a sense of empowerment, protection, and security that was denied under the law. Exacerbating matters is the ease with which blacks could obtain liquor. "As probably never before," explains Clarke, "alcohol became a way for many blacks to blur the impact of the enormous difficulties they faced."[14] What's more, Clarke notes that this deadly combination—armed, angry, and drunk—"accounts for more black lives lost in a shorter period of time than lynching and capital punishment combined."[15] Thus, there is a salient correlation between social conditions that existed post-emancipation and the existential social conditions prevalent in America's urban black communities.

David Wilson, in *Inventing Black-on-Black Violence*, argues that the increased violence involving African-Americans in U.S. cities after 1980 is perhaps predictable. Debunking the claim that African-Americans' culture is to blame for the violence (although the issue of "black culture" cannot be completely dismissed), Wilson justifies his claim by noting that oppressive living conditions—"loss of decent paying jobs, stigmatized identities and residential settings, institutional withdrawal of resources, and unabated physical decay"—that have spawned hopelessness and violence.[16] Wilson cites data collected by Michael Tonry of the University of Chicago and Norvel Morris of the University of Maryland that underscore the gravity of the epidemic. Their study concluded that homicide was the leading cause of death for black men and women between the ages of twenty-five and thirty-four; that black men from twenty-five through forty-four years old were eleven times more likely to die as homicide victims than were white men in that same age bracket; and that one of every two male murder victims was black, although one of every nine Americans was black.[17]

---

13. Ibid., 48.
14. Ibid.
15. Ibid.
16. Wilson, *Black-on-Black Violence*, ix.
17. See Tonry and Morris, *Crime and Justice*.

Life-Situation Preaching for African-Americans

Wilson observed that discussants in the black-on-black violence epidemic often focused on black cultural dysfunctionalism and the decline of youth values and attitudes rather than class, poverty, oppression, hopelessness, human denigration, economic deindustrialization, and impacts of globalization.[18] Highlighting the oppressive social conditions in inner cities, he writes:

> All [conservatives, liberals, Marxists, black separatists] agreed inner cities suffered from accelerated deterioration reflected in increased drugs (especially crack cocaine), declining living conditions, vanishing jobs, mounting youth frustration, and growing unemployment. Drug selling, drug addiction, lessened job opportunities, and economic instability were universally acknowledged as more prevalent. Selling crack cocaine, the scourge of inner cities, emerged as the new employer of youth and adults. The result was increased crime: purse snatching, car theft, assault, and murder.[19]

No commentary is necessary on this point. Simply put, black-on-black violence is the result of inextricably intertwined and interrelated racial, social and economic phenomena that have profound consequences for the African-American community, especially youths. It should serve as a reminder, not a surprise, that forces outside of the African-American community have a tangible impact on the quality of life of that community. These are the "life situations" of the African-American community to which the young African-American preacher and the church must respond courageously and creatively. A sermon that does not connect with or speak to these life situations is better left unpreached. The efficacy of the life-situation sermon for African-Americans is the sermon's ability to establish vital contact with interests and experiences of its listeners.

Rufus Burrow, Jr., in his article "Martin Luther King, Jr, Personalism, and Intracommunity Black Violence," notes that much of the intracommunity violence among young African-American males is a reaction to outside forces such as racism, white supremacy, and economic exploitation. Noting the unprecedented levels of lovelessness, hopelessness, aimlessness, and sheer mean-spiritedness among young African-American males today, Burrow reminds us that "historically there is nothing in the value system of

---

18. Wilson, *Black-on-Black Violence*, 15. One must focus on both the cultural ethos and the oppressive social and economic conditions in inner cities, thus providing a holistic approach to the problem.

19. Ibid., 15–16.

African-Americans that explains the present day low estimate of the worth and value of black personhood among so many young Black males."[20] On the contrary, he notes that historically African-Americans have had a much greater appreciation for black personhood. Part of the problem, he explains, is that young African-American males have so few alternatives or quality life-choices. This means, in Burrow's words, "that far too often no matter what choice they make the result is life-threatening rather than life-enhancing."[21] He observes further that many young African-Americans exhibit low self-esteem and sense of self, which in turn leads to a lack of respect for their peers and other persons in the community.[22] There is enduring value in Burrow's analysis, for when one cannot see the worth and value of oneself, one is blind to the worth and value of other persons.

Wilson underscores this point when he writes that in order for blacks to assault, rape, rob, and murder each other, they must internalize Eurocentric racist hostility toward themselves and internalize European contempt for the color of their skin and the physiognomy of their bodies. Wilson's point: "These Blacks must take Eurocentric lies for truth and truth for lies and act accordingly. They must see their bodies as the cause of pain and as their enemy, and consequently subject them to disrespect and murderous mutilation. They will destroy others who are clothed in a body like their own for they must be the enemy too."[23] Viewing "blackness" as the cause of pain is a corollary of self-destructive behavior, and self-destructive behavior is the consequence of little to no selflove. If, for example, one truly loves oneself (including one's culture, ancestry, and physical attributes, however imperfect they might be), she or he will love other people who resemble her or him.

Historically, many whites have valued their lives but not the lives of blacks and other people of color. But this does not put the argument on its head altogether. What the argument amounts to is our understanding of people and life and the way in which such things have been understood and interpreted historically, which is beyond the scope of this book. Suffice it to say that the sense of self-worth and self-value of persons of African descent was systematically and violently undermined from the time of slavery in this country. Sadly, many blacks capitulated to the relentless and

---

20. Burrow, Jr., "Martin Luther King," 47.
21. Ibid.
22. Ibid., 52.
23. Wilson, *Black-on-Black Violence*, 106.

Life-Situation Preaching for African-Americans

raw attacks on their personhood. If, for example, the system of slavery was based solely on an economic concept and not racism, it would not have had the enduring social, economic, cultural, educational, and psychological consequences that we see today. But, the system was founded upon the presumed racial and intellectual inferiority of African-Americans, which has persisted overtly and covertly since the first Africans were brought to Jamestown, Virginia, in 1619, to aid in the production of such lucrative crops as tobacco and, later, cotton.

Whatever the case may be, no preacher, race-ethnicity notwithstanding, can speak relevantly and intelligently to the African-American listener if the preacher is not fully conversant with the historical and existential sociocultural and socioeconomic conditions that constitute the curtailment of their quality of human and civil life. Young African-American life-situation preachers must address the low levels of self-esteem and self-worth that so adversely affects the thinking and life-choices of vast numbers of African-American males. Such preaching must get at the underlying causes of black-on-black violence and seek to bring about personal, social, and communal transformation by bringing the gospel to bear on these issues. Fosdick used personal counseling as means to better understand and help people struggling with problems. Young African-American preachers who lack insight into these issues can use personal counseling as means to educate themselves. Then, during the preparation of the sermon, they can visualize the faces—victims, offenders, and families—of those who have been affected by black-on-black violence. Personal counseling is only part of the process that leads to change.

The other part, as was the case with Fosdick, was personal counseling on a group scale. The preacher must be able to take the insights gleaned from personal counseling and think through their communal implications and practical solutions. Of course this is not all that is needed. The preacher to African-American listeners must be cognizant of the social issues in the African-American community, for such issues necessitate a culturally syntonic ecclesial and communal leader who understands the consequences of the devolution of moral character and personal ethics, as well as the underlying systemic or structural causes of the maladies in African-American communities (e.g., racism, economic exploitation and injustice).

Preaching to African-Americans' Life Situations

Race and Police Brutality

A major concern for the life-situation preacher is the problematic relationship between African-American citizens and the police. The application of excessive or deadly force against African-American citizens under the pretext of maintaining social order or, more accurately put, social dominance, is of critical import to the African-American community, and, therefore, should concern the preacher. The use of unnecessary or excessive force by police officers when engaging African-Americans—although it does not have to be physical abuse (e.g., false arrests, verbal abuse, and racial profiling)—resulting in a violation of the their civil rights is in fact bad policing. Such policing affects African-Americans disproportionately. To be sure, African-Americans, especially males, are subjected to the use of excessive force and police brutality more than any other ethnic group in America. The media is saturated daily with incidents of police shootings of African-American men and youths like Trayvon Martin, Michael Brown, Freddie Gray, Walter Scott, and Tamir Rice; and African-American females like Sandra Bland and Raynetta Turner. The power of the police to implement unjust coercive-control strategies over African-Americans is not a new social phenomenon. No reasonable person would negate the necessity of sometimes having to resort to physical force to exert control over certain situations or people, especially in instances of imminent threats to public safety. Nor would a reasonable person underestimate or undervalue the extent to which police officers must protect citizens and their property, arrest criminals, reduce and-or prevent crime, and protect other law enforcement officers. This is good policing.

In his classic work *An American Dilemma: The Negro Problem and Modern Democracy* (1944), Swedish social scientist Gunnar Myrdal discusses twentieth-century policing in the South by highlighting the problems associated with African-American/police relations.[24] Noting that African-Americans' most important public encounter is with the police, Myrdal explains that white police officers are the personification of white authority and white supremacy. The police maintain social order by enforcing social customs and caste etiquette, which become extensions of the law, associated with white power. Consequently, no perceived incident of social insubordination is inconsequential, for a breach in social customs or etiquette against one white person is considered a potential threat to

---

24. Myrdal, *American Dilemma*, 535–46.

all whites. Although some things have changed since Myrdal's classic work was published, many things have not. Disrespect and mistreatment of African-American citizens by police officers devalue the former's social standing and image in society; conversely, it also diminishes the integrity, public trust, and social image of the latter.

Undergirding this issue is the statistically untenable belief that all black males are hardened criminals, committing more crime than white males. Socioeconomic status, educational achievement, or professional credentials are not enough to protect blacks from racial profiling and the use of excessive force. The upshot, so it seems, is that: "Cultural assimilation, Ivy League degrees, and six figure incomes cannot erase the mark of Blackness or the vulnerability to sudden, unprovoked police brutality and the racist insult which it triggers."[25]

In their study of police brutality against black men, Judson L. Jeffries and James N. Upton argue compellingly that the use of excessive force against black men has far-reaching political, social, and economic ramifications for the African-American community, as well as for the country as a whole.[26] Highlighting the unforeseeable consequences of police use of excessive force, they note seven ramifications that significantly affect the African-American community, each of which is worth mentioning. First, the death of an African-American male strips the family of its patriarch and breadwinner; second, it shrinks the pool of eligible men from which African-American females can choose; third, it deprives young African-American males of fathers, father figures, and role models; fourth, it produces mental and psychological anguish for African-American men; fifth, it leads to distrust of white police officers; sixth, it has a direct bearing on how women cope with the issue of spousal abuse, making African-American women less likely to call the police for domestic disputes; and seventh, it robs the African-American community of some of its political, spiritual, and community leaders. Of course the irony here is that police officers who inflict bodily harm on the most vulnerable and disadvantaged in our society unwittingly harm their own reputations and citizen-police relations by failing to protect all American citizens.

August Vollmer, former police chief in Berkeley, California (1905–1932), summarizes the public's expectations in terms of the attributes of

---

25. Upton and Jeffries, "The Political, Social, and Economic Consequences of Police Brutality," 44.

26. Ibid. See also Judson L. Jeffries, "Police Brutality of Black Men," 115–30.

a good police officer. Employing the enviable attributes of notable biblical personalities and Abraham Lincoln, Vollmer advances the following criteria:

> The citizen expects police officers to have the wisdom of Solomon, the courage of David, the strength of Samson, the patience of Job, the leadership of Moses, the kindness of the Good Samaritan, the strategical training of Alexander, the faith of Daniel, the diplomacy of Lincoln, the tolerance of the Carpenter of Nazareth, and, finally, an intimate knowledge of every branch of the natural, biological, and social sciences. If he had all these, he *might* be a good policeman.[27]

Clearly, these attributes speak to a person of impeccable moral character and integrity. Vollmer adds that "policemen [and women] must be possessed of superior intellectual endowment, physically sound, and free from mental and nervous disorders; they must have character traits which will ensure integrity, honesty, and efficiency; their personality must command the respect and liking of their associates and of the general public."[28] Today, of course, we definitely would want to expand Vollmer's idea of the good police officer to include their awareness of and sensitivity to other systems of domination and exclusion—racism, sexism, classism, ableism, ageism, heterosexism, xenophobia, homophobia, transphobia, and so on. Sadly, too many police officers remain untrained in exercising dignity, respect, fairness, and the other attributes highlighted by Vollmer.

In sum, the life-situation preacher must understand that police brutality has had and will continue to have a profound impact on the African-American community and our nation, as it continues to be one of the most critical social and political issues of the twenty-first century for African-Americans and other communities of color. Our society needs and deserves more police officers who exercise good policing practices. What does all this mean for young and novice African-American life-situation practitioners?

---

27. Vollmer, *Police and Modern Society*, 222.
28. Ibid., 222–23.

Life-Situation Preaching for African-Americans

Preaching to African-Americans' Life Situations

Young and novice African-American preachers do well to understand their listeners' context, namely, the social, political, and economic conditions that affect black life. African-American homileticians agree that the preacher must understand the existential situation of their listeners and, as LaRue advises, forge a unique way of understanding the Bible and applying those insights in very practical ways. The definitive purpose of the life-situation sermon for African-Americans is the salvation of human personality and the transformation of their community and society. The sermon cannot lose sight of the condition of the soul nor the social conditions in which African-Americans live. Dr. Martin Luther King Jr. ably addressed this dual function of preaching: "I think that preaching should grow out of the experiences of the people. Therefore, I, as a minister, must know the problems of the people that I am pastoring."[29] Influenced by southern African-American preachers' and Walter Rauschenbusch's social gospel, King believed that the preaching ministry must show concern for the individual and the society in which the individual lives. There are a number of things for young African-American preachers to consider in order to preach effectively to their audience.

First, the preacher must be in touch with the way the forces of life—individual, social, economic, and international—affect individuals and communities. More concretely, the preacher must be cognizant of people's fears, sins, prejudices, successes, failures, doubts, sorrows, conflicts, sicknesses, diseases, and inferiorities. The preacher will need to be skilled at analyzing persons in their contexts in order to apply the gospel in relevant ways. Fundamental to sermon preparation and preaching is the basic fact that people are most interested in themselves, their own problems, and the way to solve them, as noted previously.[30] This is the paradox of preaching. That is, preachers must preach about a self-sacrificial savior to people who are preeminently concerned with their own personal and social problems. Fosdick was merely stating a truth. This is certainly not the case for all people, but it is too important to overlook. Even the most devout Christian has personal questions about her or his living. The preacher's theological and psychological awareness regarding such issues is critical to establishing

---

29. Carson, *Autobiography*, 18–19.
30. Fosdick, "What Is the Matter With Preaching?," 36.

Preaching to African-Americans' Life Situations

vital contact with African-American listeners and preaching life-transforming sermons.

The reality of meaninglessness, hopelessness, purposelessness, and lovelessness pose formidable threats to black life, and the life-situation preacher must address these destructive phenomena through effective preaching that manufactures meaning, hope, purpose, and love amongst African-Americans. For far too many African-Americans, life is overborne with nihilistic sentiments and profound despair. As noted before, effective life-situation preaching must address intracommunity violence and the inner struggle for value, meaning, and hope in a society where African-Americans have been divested of such life-forming, life-sustaining, and life-enhancing resources. An individual at peace with self can live peaceably in society.

Second, the preacher must be aware of and sensitive to the dynamics of social relationships and how the absence of such relationships in the community can disrupt personal efficiency rather than sustain and enhance it. Societal norms in urban areas can reinforce dysfunctional and destructive behaviors that bring about personal, social, and communal disruption and decimation. Thus, life-situation preaching must speak to the atrophy of values and the absence of self-love, self-respect, and love of neighbor in the African-American community, while denouncing the structural constraints that cause them. Fosdick's indispensable homiletical advice is that a sermon must bring to pass in the lives of the congregation the thing it talks about.[31] What this suggests for our contemporary setting is that a sermon on African-American life situations should create in its listeners the subject that the preacher is discussing. Thus, the life-situation sermon should not only speak to African-American listeners about self-love, self-respect, and love of neighbor; it should help produce it in them.

A sermon on love—"You Shall Love Your Neighbor as Yourself" (Matt 22:39), for example—should explain, first, self-love, and, second, love of neighbor, as it is difficult, if not impossible, to love one's neighbor without self-love. Better yet, it should produce self-love and love of neighbor in its listeners. The question that the preacher must ask is what biblical passages and relevant truths speak to the concrete and pervasive problems in the African-American community, and how can the church address these problems creatively.[32] Fosdick's life-situation preaching is helpful in this

---

31. Ibid., 37.

32. Although this chapter has been preeminently concerned with the issues in the

Life-Situation Preaching for African-Americans

regard. As noted previously, Fosdick searched for a relevant truth, turning to the Bible invariably to reinforce the aim of the sermon.

Seeking to affirm blackness, the life-situation preacher, in preparation of her sermon, must ask (1) what have I ever read in general literature—biography, history, novels, poetry—that throws light upon the problems in the African-American church and community?; (2) what have I ever run upon in personal counseling of African-Americans that illustrates the human need with which I am dealing and the resources to meet it?; (3) where, beyond the passages I have already thought of, does the Bible—that vast storehouse of experience—illumine the sermon's problem and the way to treat it for African-Americans?; (4) what, in my own personal experience as an African-American, has this intimately meant to me, and what—honest to goodness!—does it really mean now in my own life?[33] The answers to these questions provide insightful sermonic material for African-American listeners.

Edgar N. Jackson could not be more correct in his contention that "it is well within the bounds of reason to believe that in our day many who come to worship are disturbed by inner conflicts, burdened by a sense of defeat, and threatened by states of depression that can impair their efficiency as persons, though they may not lead to complete destruction."[34] The life-situation sermon, as a didactic instrument, can help African-Americans understand how their Christian faith and ethics can help them cope with the harsh realities of their existential context, inspiring a new and more profound sense of hope by helping struggling personalities overcome self-defeat and self-hate. In a word, life-situation preaching at its best applies the principles of the life-situation preaching to African-Americans' life situations in order to address the multifarious, multidimensional problems that perpetually destroy their lives and community.

Third, the preacher must understand and respond to the pervasive sense of inferiority, disaffirmation of blackness, and personal inadequacy

---

African-American community, these issues are not divorced from the black church, as the black church exists within the African-American community and consists of its people. More importantly, the black church should be as concerned with these issues as the preacher, for these issues have communal and ecclesial implications and consequences.

33. This chapter does not presume that only African-American preachers preach to African-American audiences or that only white preachers preach to white audiences. The point is that preachers who preach to African-Americans must understand their life situations.

34. Jackson, *How to Preach to People's Needs*, 84.

that many African-Americans face daily, and attempt to shore up hope and self-affirmation in human personalities so afflicted by life-depriving social forces and white supremacy. The preacher must understand the causes of these psychological and social problems before she can preach effectively to such needs. Most often such feelings are rooted in childhood or adolescent experiences. Early faulty comparisons of black youths to white youths can often result in blacks feeling inadequate because of their skin color, socioeconomic status, lack of material possessions, or educational achievement. The yearning for social recognition and acceptance under such circumstance can be mortifyingly devastating, often resulting in brokenness—broken spirits, broken hearts, broken minds, broken homes, broken families, and broken social relationships. Disconnected from society, young African-Americans facing brokenness are left without support systems that model strong moral character. The life-situation sermon should get at these issues by providing practical biblical knowledge to listeners in order to influence the way they think about themselves and other people, especially other African-Americans.

Fourth, the preacher must be able to deal constructively with injurious and pervasive attitudes and behaviors that contribute to violence and criminal activity. When used effectively and done correctly, the sermon can motivate African-Americans to believe in themselves, to set high goals, to be persons of integrity and moral character, and to respect their own lives, the lives of their neighbors, and the larger society. While it is true that adolescents go through a period of challenging moral standards and parental instruction, it is also true that the preacher can help guide and encourage adolescents as they go through their psychological odyssey of self-discovery. Early negative adolescent experiences can cause irreparable psychological damage and become an important determinant of future attitudes and actions.

In light of all this, the preacher has a critically important task, as one writer explains: "The preacher can help to encourage the development of the type of maturity that will minimize injurious behavior by giving insights to parents of adolescents, on the one hand, so that this period of growth can be accepted with as much mutual understanding as possible."[35] The absence of moral standards, familial support, and social ties can lead to a categorical rejection of American social life. Despised, dejected, and rejected, too many African-American youths find refuge, security, and

---

35. Ibid., 144.

Life-Situation Preaching for African-Americans

affirmation in the black underbelly of American society, thus becoming inveterate criminals and troublemakers. The underbelly of society may appear appealing to socially rejected youths, as it provides an opportunity for social acceptance and recognition through a spurious sense of physical courage and respect otherwise denied them.

Finally, the preacher must help young black males better understand how they feel about themselves and why they feel the way they do, thus helping them to control any compulsive appetite for violence and crime. Such an attitude is often linked to the need for love, self-affirmation, and emotional support. In addition, the preacher must counter the psychological consequences of crippling social and economic conditions that breed despair and an inferiority complex. Aware of the dynamics of low self-esteem or no self-esteem, parents can be instrumental in shoring up moral standards, ethics, and the affirmation of black humanity in order to breed hope, self-esteem, and self-love.[36] By preaching sermons that address both the parents and children, the preacher imputes knowledge that facilitates self-love and self-correction of destructive attitudes and behaviors.

The life-situation sermon must help people see themselves and their possibilities more clearly. This has the value of helping them to see and understand the inadequacy of their thoughts and feelings about themselves, and better comprehend the dignity and worth of human personality. The life-situation sermon can be instrumental in helping African-American listeners understand their importance as children of God created in God's glorious image. Every person is important to God. Period. For this reason, the sermon should help persons to see themselves as God sees them, thereby developing an image of self that is compatible with God's. The preacher who is helping African-Americans to understand the depths of their attitudes, actions, and behaviors is performing a vital task; that is, she or he is helping listeners come to grips with their injurious behavior in order to correct and prevent such behavior.

One's special circumstance and social environment do not by themselves determine the quality or potentiality of one's life, although they contribute substantively, for what one chooses to be is to a large degree a matter of discipline, intestinal fortitude, hope beyond visible realities and crippling setbacks, self-affirmation, and self-love. The importance of hope is not to be understated. "When man thinks of himself as beyond hope, needing

---

36. In *Preaching for Black Self-Esteem*, Mitchell and Thomas provide superlative examples of sermons designed to increase black self-esteem.

Preaching to African-Americans' Life Situations

change but fundamentally incorrigible, he drowns himself in despair,"[37] notes Samuel M. Shoemaker. Who a woman is and where she is today is not indicative of who she will be or where she will be tomorrow. The life-situation sermon must produce this kind of courageous faith, which is supremely rooted in God's ability to create infinite possibilities for the disadvantaged in the face of seemingly insurmountable life situations. The gospel of Mark informs us that our belief creates unlimited possibilities, for "If you are able!—All things can be done for the one who believes" (9:23).

Life-situation preaching at its best condemns black-on-black violence while calling attention to the social, economic, political, and educational conditions that cause and perpetuate its existence. That is, the preacher condemns the destructive forces, attitudes, and behaviors internal and external to the African-American community. The preacher is not merely concerned with treating the symptoms, but rather, even more so, the underlying causes of the problems. The effective life-situation sermon helps African-American listeners to overcome the nagging sense of inferiority foisted on them by white America and to face their devitalizing social conditions with unconditional love for God, themselves, their community, and their world. Life-situation preaching is an indispensable homiletical tool to help reshape the spiritual, personal, social, moral, and ethical life of African-Americans; as such, it can help bring about resilient and robust personalities who are able to cope with and overcome the problems they face on a daily basis.

---

37. Shoemaker, *How To Become A Christian*, 52.

Bibliography

Allen, Ronald J., Barbara Shires Blaisdell, and Scott Black Johnston. *Theology for Preaching: Authority, Truth, and Knowledge of God in A Postmodern Ethos*. Nashville: Abingdon, 1997.
Beverly, Harry Black. *Harry Emerson Fosdick's Predigtweise, Its Significance (for America), Its Limits, Its Overcoming*. Winterthur, Switzerland: Keller, 1965.
Broadus, John A. *On The Preparation and Delivery of Sermons*. New York: Harper & Row, 1944.
Brooks, Phillips. *Lectures on Preaching*. New York: Dutton, 1877.
Bryson, Harold T. and James C. Taylor. *Building Sermons To Meet People's Needs*. Nashville: Broadman, 1980.
Burrow, Rufus, Jr. "Martin Luther King, Jr, Personalism, and Intracommunity Black Violence." *Encounter* 58 (1997) 41–60.
Buttrick, David. "A Fearful Pulpit, A Wayward Land." In *What's The Matter with Preaching Today?*, edited by Mike Graves, 37–50. Louisville: Westminster John Knox, 2004.
Cannon, Katie G. *Teaching Preaching: Isaac Rufus Clark and Black Sacred Rhetoric*. New York: The Continuum International, 2002.
Carson, Clayborne, ed. *The Autobiography of Martin Luther King, Jr*. New York: Warner, 1998.
Carson, Clayborne, et al. *The Papers of Martin Luther King, Jr*. Vol. VI, *Advocate of the Social Gospel, September 1948–March 1963*. Berkeley: University of California Press, 2000.
———. *The Papers of Martin Luther King, Jr*. Vol. IV, *Symbol of the Movement, January 1957–December 1958*. Berkeley: University of California Press, 2000.
Cauthen, Kenneth. *The Impact of American Religious Liberalism*. New York: Harper & Row, 1962.
Clarke, James W. "Black-on-Black Violence." *Society* 33.5 (1996) 46–50.
Coffin, Henry Sloane. *A Half Century of Union Theological Seminary: An Informal History*. New York: Scribner, 1954.
Conn, Joanne Wolski, ed. *Women's Spirituality: Resources for Christian Development*. 1986. Reprint, Eugene, OR: Wipf & Stock, 2005.
———. "The Rhetorical Theory of Harry Emerson Fosdick." In *Harry Emerson Fosdick's Art of Preaching*, edited by Lionel Crocker, 228–35. Springfield, IL: Thomas, 1971.
Craddock, Fred B. *Preaching*. Nashville: Abingdon, 1985.
Davis, Angela J., ed. *Policing the Black Man: Arrest, Prosecution, and Imprisonment*. New York: Pantheon, 2017.

Bibliography

DuBois, W. E. B. "The Religion of the American Negro." In *W. E. B. DuBois on Sociology and the Black Community*, edited by Dan S. Green and Edwin D. Driver, 214–25. Chicago: University of Chicago Press, 1978.

Edwards, O. C., Jr. *A History of Preaching*. Nashville: Abingdon, 2004.

Forbes, James. *The Holy Spirit and Preaching*. Nashville: Abingdon, 1989.

Fosdick, Harry Emerson. "Animated Conversation." In *Harry Emerson Fosdick's Art of Preaching*, edited by Lionel Crocker, 47–50. Springfield, IL: Thomas, 1971.

———. *As I See Religion*. New York: Harper, 1932.

———. *The Autobiography of Harry Emerson Fosdick: The Living of These Days*. New York: Harper, 1965.

———. "The Christian Ministry." In *Harry Emerson Fosdick's Art of Preaching: An Anthology*, edited by Lionel Crocker, 58–68. Springfield, IL: Thomas, 1971.

———. *Christianity and Progress*. New York: Association Press, 1922.

———. *A Faith for Tough Times*. New York: Harper, 1952.

———. *A Great Time To Be Alive*. New York: Harper, 1944.

———. *A Guide to Understanding the Bible*. New York: Harper, 1938.

———. "How I Prepare My Sermons." In *Harry Emerson Fosdick's Art of Preaching*, edited by Lionel Crocker, 42–46. Springfield, IL: Thomas, 1971.

———. "The Ideas That Use Us." In *The Power to See It Through: Sermons on Christianity Today*, Harry Emerson Fosdick, 171–79. New York: Harper, 1935.

———. "Learning to Preaching." In *Harry Emerson Fosdick's Art of Preaching: An Anthology*, edited by Lionel Crocker, 5–26. Springfield, IL: Thomas, 1971.

———. "A Modern Preacher's Problem in His Use of the Scriptures." Inaugural address at Union Theological Seminary. September 30, 1915.

———. *The Modern Use of the Bible*. New York: Macmillan, 1924.

———. *On Being A Real Person*. New York: Harper, 1943.

———. "Personal Counseling and Preaching." In *Harry Emerson Fosdick's Art of Preaching*, edited by Lionel Crocker, 51–57. Springfield, IL: Thomas, 1971.

———. *The Power to See It Through: Sermons on Christianity Today*. New York: Harper, 1935.

———. "To Those Interested in the Profession of Ministry." In *Harry Emerson Fosdick's Art of Preaching: An Anthology*, edited by Lionel Crocker, 69–72. Springfield, IL: Thomas, 1971.

———. "What Is the Matter With Preaching." In *Harry Emerson Fosdick's Art of Preaching: An Anthology*, edited by Lionel Crocker, 27–41. Springfield, IL: Thomas, 1971.

Fry Brown, Teresa L. *Delivering the Sermon: Voice, Body, and Animation in Proclamation*. Minneapolis: Fortress, 2008.

———. *Weary Throats and New Songs: Black Women Proclaiming Gods Word*. Nashville: Abingdon, 2003.

Holmes, Malcolm D., and Brad W. Smith. *Race and Police Brutality: Roots of an Urban Dilemma*. Albany: State University of New York Press, 2008.

Jackson, Edgar N. *How to Preach People's Needs*. Nashville: Abingdon, 1956.

Jeffries, Judson L. "Police Brutality of Black Men and the Destruction of the African-American Community." *The Negro Educational Review* 52.4 (2001) 115–30.

Johnston, Graham. *Preaching to a Postmodern World*. Grand Rapids: Baker, 2001.

Jones, Edgar DeWitt. *The Royalty of the Pulpit*. New York: Harper, 1951.

Kemp, Charles F. *Life-Situation Preaching*. St. Louis: Bethany, 1956.

Killinger, John. *Fundamentals of Preaching*. 2nd ed. Minneapolis: Fortress, 1996.

Bibliography

Kitchens, Jim. *The Postmodern Parish: New Ministry for a New Era.* Lanham, MD: Rowman & Littlefield, 2003.

LaRue, Cleophus J. *The Heart of Black Preaching.* Louisville: Westminster John Knox, 2000.

———. *I Believe I'll Testify: The Art of African American Preaching.* Louisville: Westminster John Knox, 2011.

———. *Power in the Pulpit: How America's Most Effective Black Preachers Prepare Their Sermons.* Louisville: Westminster John Knox, 2002.

———. "Two Ships Passing in the Night." In *What's The Matter With Preaching Today?*, edited by Mike Graves, 127–44. Louisville: Westminster John Knox, 2004.

Lincoln, Eric, and Lawrence H. Mamiya. *The Black Church in the African American Experience.* Durham: Duke University Press, 1990.

Linn, Edmund Holt. *Preaching as Counseling: The Unique Method of Harry Emerson Fosdick.* Valley Forge, PA: Judson, 1966.

———. "Harry Emerson and the Techniques of Organization." In *Harry Emerson Fosdick's Art of Preaching: An Anthology*, edited by Lionel Crocker, 186–209. Springfield, IL: Thomas, 1971.

Lischer, Richard. *A Theology of Preaching: The Dynamics of the Gospel.* Abingdon Preacher's Library. Nashville: Abingdon, 1981.

———. *The Preacher King.* New York: Oxford University Press, 1995.

Macnab, John B. "Fosdick at First Church." In *A Preaching Ministry: Twenty-One Sermons Preached by Harry Emerson Fosdick At the First Presbyterian Church in the City of New York, 1918-1925*, edited by David Pultz, 20–49. New York: The First Presbyterian Church, 2000.

Massey, James Earl. *Designing the Sermon: Order and Movement in Preaching.* Nashville: Abingdon, 1980.

May, Eugene. "How Dr. Fosdick Uses the Bible in Preaching." In *Harry Emerson Fosdick's Art of Preaching: An Anthology*, edited by Lionel Crocker, 80–85. Springfield, IL: Thomas, 1971.

McCracken, Robert J. *The Making of the Sermon.* New York: Harper & Brothers, 1956.

McGrath, Alister E. *Christian Theology: An Introduction.* Malden, MA: Blackwell, 2007.

McMickle, Marvin A. *Shaping the Claim: Moving from Text to Sermon.* Minneapolis: Fortress, 2008.

Miller, Keith D. *Voice of Deliverance: The Language of Martin Luther King Jr. and Its Sources.* New York: Free Press, 1992.

Miller, Roberts Moats. *Harry Emerson Fosdick: Preacher, Pastor, Prophet.* New York: Oxford University Press, 1985.

Mitchell, Henry H. *Black Preaching: The Recovery of A Powerful Art.* Nashville: Abingdon, 1990.

Mitchell, Henry H., and Emil M. Thomas. *Preaching for Black Self-Esteem.* Nashville: Abingdon, 1994.

Myrdal, Gunnar. *An American Dilemma: The Negro Problem and Modern Democracy.* New York: Harper, 1944.

Niebuhr, Reinhold. "The significance of Dr. Fosdick in American Religious Thought." *Union Seminary Quarterly Review* 8.4 (1953) 3–6.

Osteen, Joel. *Your Best Life Now: 7 Steps to Living at Your Full Potential.* New York: Faith Works, 2004.

Bibliography

Palley, Howard A., and Dana A. Robinson. "Black on Black Crime." *Society* 25.5 (1988) 59–62.

Plant, E. Ashby, and B. Michelle Peruche. "The Consequences of Race for Police Officers' Responses to Criminal Suspects." *Psychological Science* 16.3 (2005) 180–83.

Pultz, David, ed. *A Preaching Ministry: Twenty-One Sermons Preached by Harry Emerson Fosdick at the First Presbyterian Church in the City of New York, 1918–1925.* New York: First Presbyterian Church, 2000.

Ruopp, Harold W. "Life Situation Preaching" (2 parts). In *The Christian Century Pulpit* Vol. XII, No. 12.5 (1941) 116–17, 140–41.

Ryan, Halford R. *Harry Emerson Fosdick: Persuasive Preacher.* New York: Greenwood, 1989.

———. "A Preacher Preaching." In *A Preaching Ministry: Twenty-One Sermons by Harry Emerson Fosdick At the First Presbyterian Church in the City of New York, 1918–1925*, edited by David Pultz, 50–65. New York: The First Presbyterian Church, 2000.

Sanders, J. Oswald. *Spiritual Leadership.* Chicago: Moody, 2007.

Shoemaker, Samuel M. *How To Become a Christian.* New York: Harper & Brothers, 1953.

Simmons, Martha, and Frank A. Thomas, eds. *Preaching with Sacred Fire: An Anthology of African American Sermons, 1750 to the Present.* New York: Norton, 2010.

Taylor, Barbara Brown. *The Preaching Life.* Cambridge, MA: Cowley, 1993.

Taylor, Gardner C. "Building the Sermon." In *The Words of Gardner Taylor*, vol. 5, edited by Edward L. Taylor, 171–83. Pennsylvania: Judson, 2001.

———. "Contemporary Preaching." In *The Words of Gardner Taylor*, vol. 5, edited by Edward L. Taylor, 96–99. Valley Forge, PA: Judson, 2001.

———. "Preaching in the Urban Situation." In *The Words of Gardner Taylor*, Vol. 5, edited by Edward L. Taylor, 89–95. Valley Forge, PA: Judson, 2001.

———. "The Preaching of the Black Patriarchs, Part 2." In *The Words of Gardner Taylor*, Vol. 5, edited by Edward L. Taylor, 209–218. Valley Forge, PA: Judson, 2001.

———. "Preaching the Whole Counsel of God." In *The Words of Gardner Taylor*, Vol. 5, edited by Edward L. Taylor, 184–196. Valley Forge, PA: Judson, 2001.

———. "Reflections on the Preaching Responsibility." In *The Words of Gardner Taylor*, Vol. 5, edited by Edward L. Taylor, 100–112. Valley Forge, PA: Judson, 2001.

———. "Shaping Sermons by the Shape of Text and Preacher." In *The Words of Gardner Taylor*, Vol. 5, edited by Edward L. Taylor, 43–49. Valley Forge, PA: Judson, 2001.

Thomas, Frank A. *They Like to Never Quit Praisin' God: The Role of Celebration in Preaching.* Cleveland: United Church, 1997.

———. *Introduction to the Practice of African American Preaching.* Nashville: Abingdon, 2016.

Thompson, Lisa L. *Ingenuity: Preaching as an Outsider.* Nashville: Abingdon, 2018.

Thurman, Howard. *Jesus and the Disinherited.* Boston: Beacon, 1976.

Tisdale, Leonora Tubbs. *Preaching as Local Theology and Folk Art.* Fortress Resources for Preaching. Minneapolis: Fortress, 1997.

———. *Prophetic Preaching: A Pastoral Approach.* Louisville: Westminster John Knox, 2010.

Tonry, Michael and Norvel Morris. *Crime and Justice.* Chicago: University of Chicago Press, 1984.

Upton, James N. and Judson L. Jeffries. "The Political, Social, and Economic Consequences of Police Brutality Against Black Men." *The Griot* 26.2 (2007) 43–52.

Bibliography

Vines, Jerry, and Jim Shaddix. *Power in the Pulpit: How to Prepare and Deliver Expository Sermons*. Chicago: Moody, 1999.

Vollmer, August. *The Police and Modern Society*. 1936. Reprint, Montclair, NJ: Patterson Smith, 1971.

Warren, Mervyn A. *King Came Preaching: The Pulpit Power of Dr. Martin Luther King Jr.* Downers Grove, IL: InterVarsity, 2001.

Willimon, William H. *Integrative Preaching: The Pulpit at the Center*. Abingdon Preacher's Library. Nashville: Abingdon, 1981.

Willimon, William H., and Richard Lischer, eds. *Concise Encyclopedia of Preaching*. Louisville: Westminster John Knox, 1995.

Wilson, David. *Inventing Black-on-Black Violence*. Syracuse: Syracuse University Press, 2005.

Wilson, Amos N. *Black-on-Black Violence: The Psychodynamics of Black Self-Annihilation In Service of White Domination*. Brooklyn: Afrikan World InfoSystems, 1990.